Navigating Paul
An Introduction to Key Theological Concepts

Jouette M. Bassler

Westminster John Knox Press
LOUISVILLE • LONDON

Scripture quotations, unless otherwise indicated, are from the New Revised Standard Version of the Bible, copyright © 1989 by the Division of Christian Education of the National Council of the Churches of Christ in the U.S.A., and used by permission.

Book design by Sharon Adams
Cover design by Night & Day Design

First edition
Published by Westminster John Knox Press
Louisville, Kentucky

This book is printed on acid-free paper that meets the American National Standards Institute Z39.48 standard.⊗

PRINTED IN THE UNITED STATES OF AMERICA

07 08 09 10 11 12 13 14 15 16 — 10 9 8 7 6 5 4 3 2 1

Library of Congress Cataloging-in-Publication Data

Bassler, Jouette M.
  Navigating Paul : an introduction to key theological concepts / Jouette M. Bassler. — 1st ed.
        p. cm.
  Includes bibliographical references and indexes.
  ISBN-13: 978-0-664-22741-8 (alk. paper)
  ISBN-10: 0-664-22741-4 (alk. paper)
  1. Bible. N.T. Epistles of Paul — Theology. I. Title.
  BS2652.B38 2007
  227'.06—dc22

                                                                    2006048986

Navigating Paul

For my students, from whom I have learned so much

Contents

Preface

This is not a book on Paul's theology. I am not at all certain that he had "a theology," that is, a reasonably well ordered and integrated set of beliefs. Even if he did, I am not convinced that it would have remained constant over the course of his tumultuous life or that we could hope to recover it from the few and focused letters that remain of his correspondence. Clearly, though, Paul did *practice* theology. That is, he thought through the problems afflicting his churches in light of the gospel; and in doing so he referred frequently to concepts of obvious theological importance: grace, faith, righteousness, and the like. What he meant by these references has been the source of much debate.

This collection of essays is intended to orient the interested reader of Paul to the significance of these concepts and the contours of the debates. The range of topics covered is not at all comprehensive, but it does include the issues that, in my judgment, most affect one's grasp of the apostle's thought. My goal has not been to simplify his thought for the reader. If anything, these essays should make it seem more complex. Recognizing this complexity, however, is crucial, both for reaching new insights into his meaning and for understanding the basis of the current debates.

Some time ago I was encouraged by Greg Glover at WJK to expand an earlier essay on grace into a glossary of Paul's theological vocabulary. My response to that suggestion has taken a somewhat different direction. The essays are much too long to be labeled a "glossary," but no mere glossary could convey the rich possibilities and shifting nuances of Paul's language. Furthermore, only a limited number of topics are covered. Even so, there is some redundancy, for explaining the meaning of Paul's references to one topic usually requires discussing the meaning of his references to another. Still, each essay is intended to be comprehensible on its own, but each is also intended to be enhanced by the others. All together, the essays will not provide a full roadmap to Paul's letters, much less to his theology, but they will provide navigational guides to the more difficult currents of his thought.

Chapter 1, "Grace: Probing Its Limits," was originally published in *Interpretation* 57.1 (2003): 24–32. It is reprinted here with permission in slightly revised form.

Abbreviations

AB	Anchor Bible
ABD	*Anchor Bible Dictionary*, ed. D. N. Freedman. 6 vols. New York: Doubleday, 1992
ANTC	Abingdon New Testament Commentaries
AT	author's translation
BBR	*Bulletin for Biblical Research*
Bib	*Biblica*
BJRL	*Bulletin of the John Rylands Library*, Manchester
BTB	*Biblical Theology Bulletin*
BZNW	Beihefte zur Zeitschrift für die neutestamentliche Wissenschaft
CBQ	*Catholic Biblical Quarterly*
ET	English translation
HDR	Harvard Dissertations in Religion
HNTC	Harper's New Testament Commentaries
HTKNT	Herders theologischer Kommentar zum Neuen Testament
HTR	*Harvard Theological Review*
HTS	Harvard Theological Studies
ICC	International Critical Commentary
Int	*Interpretation*
ISFCJ	International Studies in Formative Christianity and Judaism
JBL	*Journal of Biblical Literature*
JSJ	*Journal for the Study of Judaism*
JSNT	*Journal for the Study of the New Testament*
JSNTSup	Journal for the Study of the New Testament, Supplements

JTS	*Journal of Theological Studies*
KJV	King James (Authorized) Version
LD	Lection divina
NAB	New American Bible
NASB	New American Standard Bible
NCB	New Century Bible
Neot	*Neotestamentica*
NICNT	New International Commentary on the New Testament
NIGTC	New International Greek Testament Commentary
NIV	New International Version
NJB	New Jerusalem Bible
NovTSup	Novum Testamentum, Supplements
NRSV	New Revised Standard Version
NTS	*New Testament Studies*
OBT	Overtures to Biblical Theology
REB	Revised English Bible
SBLDS	Society of Biblical Literature Dissertation Series
SBLSymS	Society of Biblical Literature Symposium Series
SBT	Studies in Biblical Theology
SFSHJ	South Florida Studies in the History of Judaism
SNTSMS	Society for New Testament Studies Monograph Series
SP	Sacra pagina
TDNT	*Theological Dictionary of the New Testament*, ed. G. Kittel and G. Friedrich. 10 vols. Grand Rapids: Eerdmans, 1964–1976
WBC	Word Biblical Commentary
WTJ	*Westminster Theological Journal*
WUNT	Wissenschaftliche Untersuchungen zum Neuen Testament
ZTK	*Zeitschrift für Theologie und Kirche*

Chapter One

GRACE

Probing Its Limits

I t is significantly harder to write on the Pauline concept of grace now than it was twenty, fifteen, or even ten years ago. The general agreement about the basic structure of Paul's theology that prevailed not too many years ago has collapsed and been replaced by the chaos of vigorous debate.[1] In that debate, even old certitudes about grace, that most characteristic component of Paul's theology, have been shaken. Few would deny the basic premise that grace is central to Paul's thought,[2] but few would also now deny that grace was central to almost all forms of first-century Judaism. Furthermore, with the blinders of old assumptions removed, it has become clear that Paul, no less than his Jewish contemporaries, affirmed not *sola gratia* in the strict sense of the words but grace *and* a judgment according to deeds.[3] And so new questions emerge: In what ways are Paul's views on grace distinctive? And against what views was his most polemical grace-language directed?

Grace All Around

Since the publication of E. P. Sanders's landmark study of Palestinian Judaism, old dogmas about Jewish legalism have become difficult to sustain.[4] Tackling the pervasive image of first-century Judaism as a legalistic (i.e., works-based) religion that left its adherents struggling to earn salvation under a grace-less code of merits, Sanders demonstrated that the primary texts of Palestinian Judaism reveal no such thing. He found a pattern of religion in which obedience to the law was of undeniable importance, but this obedience was framed, defined, and sustained by initiatives of divine grace.[5]

Israel's covenant relationship with God was, after all, established not by merit but through election, an act of pure grace, and salvation was assured to those within the covenant. To be sure, obedience to the law—or intent to obey the law—was required to *maintain* one's status within the covenant. This obedience was not, however, measured against a rigid system of merits and demerits. What was expected was faithfulness, not perfection, and God's grace was manifested again through divine forgiveness and in the provision of means of atonement for those who repented of their transgressions.

In the sectarian Judaism identified with the Dead Sea Scrolls, the impact of grace on the individual is even more pronounced. Because the sectary was not born into the community of the new covenant but joined through an act of repentance, there is a deeper sense of the individual, not the nation, as the object of election grace in these writings. And the role of grace in overcoming human sinfulness and enabling fulfillment of the law is more pronounced (as is the demand for obedience): "For Thou knowest the inclination of Thy servant, that I have not relied [upon the works of my hands] to raise up [my heart]. . . . I have no fleshly refuge; [and Thy servant has] no righteous deeds to deliver him from the [Pit of no] forgiveness. But I lean on the abun[dance of Thy mercies] and hope [for the greatness] of Thy grace, that Thou wilt bring [salvation] to flower."[6]

Much of this sounds, of course, like Paul (as more than one commentator has observed),[7] which serves to underscore the fact that the language of grace and an active religious concept of grace were well established in Paul's world.[8] The apostle had a rich tradition upon which to draw, and much that he had to say about grace, though of profound theological significance, was not theologically distinctive. Thus, for example, the numerous Pauline references to undeserved acts of divine favor or kindness—whether in calling, choosing, or justifying—reflected, in a Christ-centered key, ideas current in first-century Judaism.[9] It is valid to distinguish between a static view of election grace characteristic of those groups into which one is born, and a dynamic view characteristic of groups to which one is converted.[10] Even the former, however, possessed a dynamic sense of forgiving grace and an active piety resting on it.

The opposition of sin and grace is a complex matter. Certainly in first-century Judaism divine forgiveness and means of atonement were understood as manifestations of God's grace, and certainly this forgiveness-grace was understood to be sufficient for every transgression.[11] Thus Paul's claim that "where sin increased, grace abounded all the more"

(Rom 5:20) would not be incomprehensible within the framework of Jewish thought. Yet Paul goes further. As he begins to describe sin, no longer in terms of transgressions but as a power exercising absolute control over human lives (Rom 5–7), he moves beyond typical Jewish understanding.[12] His comments on grace develop along similar lines ("grace might also exercise dominion," Rom 5:21; see also 6:14–15); and here too he moves beyond typical Jewish expression. But the differences are more of degree than of substance. Paul had a more pessimistic view of human nature than most of his Jewish contemporaries,[13] evoking a more powerful image of divine grace. Yet Paul's presentation of the sin-grace dichotomy as an opposition of powerful forces can be seen as an extension of traditional Jewish confidence in the ability of divine grace to overcome sins. It does not represent an altogether new development in the concept of grace.[14]

Yet that is not the complete picture. Paul's understanding of grace was not only rooted in his Jewish world; it was also shaped by his encounter with Jesus, by his struggles with his churches, and by his subsequent theological reflection. Thus in his discussions of suffering and the law, grace acquires distinctive overtones characteristic of his thought alone.

The Grace of Suffering

First-century Judaism knew of a connection between grace and suffering.[15] Suffering could be understood as the grace-filled means by which God led persons to repentance. Suffering could also be seen as the God-given means for individuals to atone for their sins in this world, thereby preserving for themselves a reward in the world to come. In some circles the suffering of righteous martyrs was held to make amends for the sins of others. For Paul, though, the connection was entirely different. He embraced, of course, the conviction of the early church that all the grace of atonement was concentrated in the once-for-all event of the cross (Rom 3:24–25)[16]—Jesus' death "for us" or "on our behalf" (Greek *hyper hēmōn*, Rom 5:8)—which made amends for human sins.[17] Yet Paul could also say to the Philippians, "[God] has graciously granted you the privilege not only of believing in Christ, *but of suffering for him as well*" (Phil 1:29).[18] Grace was involved not only in Christ's death for them, but also in their suffering "for Christ" (Greek *hyper Christou*). But how was that possible? And how was it "grace"? We need to look at the context of this statement in Philippians.

Paul knew and expressed various understandings of human suffering.[19]

He knew—because he experienced it—that God provides the power to endure suffering (1 Thess 1:6; 2 Cor 1:3–11; 4:7–12). He knew also—because it was revealed to him (2 Cor 12:7–10)—that when God's power is exercised through human instruments, it is most clearly known to be *God's* power when those instruments are themselves most obviously without power of their own. So suffering is the lot of the apostle, in order that God's power may be perfectly revealed (1 Cor 2:1–5; 2 Cor 4:7; 13:1–4). But in Phil 1:29 grace is apparently connected with the suffering itself, not with the power to endure it or with the divine power revealed in it.

To be sure, those other ideas are present in the verses that precede this one, for there Paul asserts that the Philippians' steadfastness and courage in the face of opposition is evidence of God working in them, a sign of their salvation (vv. 27–28). But when he continues his thought in verse 29, he seems to move in a different direction. Here the emphasis is on the suffering itself, and it is the fact that the suffering is "for Christ" or "on behalf of Christ" that is God's gracious gift.[20] But in what way is *their* suffering on *his* behalf?

Like Paul, the Philippian church was experiencing persecution (1:28), though of what sort or what severity we do not know. They were most assuredly, however, suffering persecution as followers of Christ and in that sense "on his behalf." In a world hostile to followers of Christ, the gift of faith was at the same time the "gift" of suffering. But Paul means much more than that. For Paul, believing in Christ meant believing *into* Christ.[21] When believers were baptized they were baptized *into* Christ (Gal 3:27), into Christ's body (1 Cor 12:13), into Christ's death (Rom 6:3). These were not simply metaphors for joining the church, but described the reality of joining with Christ. The life of the faithful was life in union with Christ. It was "knowing" Christ by participating in Christ, which included sharing in his suffering in their daily lives (2 Cor 4:10–11) and experiencing there the power of his resurrection as well—*both* suffering *and* resurrection power, not one or the other.[22] Suffering was part of the gracious gift of knowing Christ fully—a gift not just for Paul but also for all who were united with Christ in faith and baptism.

Moreover, in this particular passage the grace of their suffering is identified with "the same struggle" that Paul himself was enduring (Phil 1:30), a struggle linked not simply with belief in Christ or identification with Christ, but more specifically with proclamation of Christ (1:7, 16). An important part of the gracious privilege of suffering for Christ that the Philippians shared with Paul was the privilege of suffering for the proclamation of the gospel. Indeed, their suffering *was* the proclamation of the gospel, for Paul describes the gospel to which and for which they were graciously called as the gospel of the crucified Christ (1 Cor 1:23; 2:2; Gal 6:14; see also Phil 3:18; Gal 3:1). This gospel is embedded and embodied in the lives of believers (Phil 3:10–11); it is proclaimed through the lives of believers, insofar as their lives manifest not only the power of the resurrection but also—and especially—the suffering of the cross. The Philippians, Paul says, have thus been graciously privileged to share in the proclamation of the gospel of the crucified Christ through their lives. They are to understand their suffering as a gift, not because it has atoning value—only Christ's death could accomplish that—or because it leads them to repentance, but because it marks their union with Christ and, like the eucharistic meal, proclaims his death until he returns (1 Cor 11:26).

This identification of grace with human suffering is a message both profound and disturbing. Paul instructs the Philippians to find evidence of God's favor or grace not in power or prestige that sets them above others, but in suffering that unites them with others and promotes humility. This is a message that Paul develops at greatest length when writing to churches that tended toward (or had a significant number of members that tended toward) selfish ambition and inflated self-esteem.[23] It is, however, a message that carries significant risk in its contemporary application. Through it those who are weak and suffering can find meaning in their suffering, but they will find no critique of the causes of that suffering, no encouragement to resist or to overcome it.[24] It is a message that encourages humility—an important message for those inclined toward arrogance and greed, but a devastating one for those pushed by others into lives of humiliation and self-denial.[25] The crucial words "on behalf of Christ" can buffer the equation against gross misuse, and the reminder that the gracious favor of participation in Christ also includes participation in his resurrection power prevents the gift of suffering from being linked with any form of self-abasement. But experience has shown that the danger of misapplication is real, and we do well to remember that there are circumstances when suffering on behalf of Christ is not appropriately presented as part of God's gracious gift.

Grace against the Law

The most distinctive understanding of grace to emerge in the Pauline letters, and the one most closely identified with Paul, is found exclusively in Romans and Galatians, where grace stands in stark opposition to the law or works of law: "You who want to be justified by the law have cut your-selves off from Christ; you have fallen away from grace" (Gal 5:4; see also 1:6; 2:21; Rom 3:24; 4:16; 6:14, 15; 11:6). Such a thought was inconceiv-able in Judaism, where obedience to the law was conducted within a framework of grace. In these letters the term "grace" has clearly acquired a new connotation, but there is no consensus over its precise nuance, for there is no agreement over what Paul means by the opposing term "law" (or "works of law").

For Rudolf Bultmann, the law (as Paul construes it) reveals the basic human perversion of self-reliance. Encountered as God's obligatory demand carrying the threat of judgment, the law inevitably evokes the sin-ful response of "self-powered striving . . . to procure salvation by [one's] own strength."[26] Paul's objection to the law, then, is not directed against the difficulty of fulfilling its demands. It is directed against the system of works-righteousness (legalism) that the law supports, a system that feeds the sin of self-achievement and generates an attitude of boastful arrogance and self-righteousness. Over against this system of perverse striving stands grace, the pure gift of deliverance from judgment. With God tak-ing the initiative by offering this gift freely, there is no room for human achievement, no basis for false pride. There can only be a response of obe-dient self-surrender.

Bultmann's interpretation is a magisterial theological achievement of stunning scope and compelling power. It is also, however, almost certainly wrong. It imposes on Paul the concerns of the Reformation and a mod-ern existentialist analysis of the human condition. Moreover, it grotesquely misrepresents first-century Judaism as a religion of "rebel-lious pride."[27] Some continue to affirm this interpretation (though elim-inating its anti-Jewish tone),[28] but it no longer dominates the field. Indeed, no single interpretation dominates the field. Instead, a range of plausible options exist that differ widely in their appraisal of the problem Paul sees with the law and thus also in the implications of opposing grace.

One option works with a view of legalism stripped of the objectionable features of pride and self-righteousness.[29] It is possible to view the law as God's revealed will and understand salvation to be conditioned on obedi-ence without concluding that obedience is always and necessarily an act of self-striving. Obedience could, for example, derive from a sincere desire to please God or to demonstrate one's faithfulness to the covenant. But if this is closer to Paul's understanding of Judaism, what is the basis for Paul's objection? To what is grace opposed? Some suggest that the problem is one of human failure: "Paul thus believes that humans do not and (apparently) cannot obey God's commandments in a way that satisfies divine requirements."[30] "Grace," then, "is the obvious antidote to the plight which resulted from life 'under law.'"[31] If the old system that was centered on the law failed because of human inability to keep the law adequately, the new covenant eliminates law and works of law from any role in salvation: all is by grace.[32]

In contrast to Bultmann's interpretation, this "softer" understanding of legalism does not fault the Jews for attempting to obey the law, but for failing to recognize their inability to succeed and their consequent need to rely on grace instead.[33] Nevertheless, it still rests on a distorted view of Judaism, for it ignores completely the important roles of human repentance and divine forgiveness in that religion.

A variant proposal frames the issue more radically. It is not that human weakness renders the law-based system impossible to satisfy; rather, God's new act in Christ renders the law-based system obsolete. Grace has invaded the world on the cross, a new principle of salvation has arrived, and to continue to rely on the law as the way to salvation is to fail to recognize that the rules have changed.[34] With the advent of Christ, salvation is by grace, not by works of the law.

While this understanding of the law-grace dichotomy does better justice to Paul's apocalyptic way of thinking,[35] it still rests on a distorted picture of Judaism. If Sanders is right (as I think he is), first-century Judaism understood well that salvation was by grace and did not regard it as something to be earned by works of the law. This proposal can therefore be maintained only by noting that the law-grace dichotomy is artificial, based either on a mistake by Paul[36] or on his questionable decision to misrepresent Judaism in order to buttress his argument.[37] Neither choice is particularly appealing.

A third proposal takes a different starting point. It proceeds from the assumption that in setting grace against the law Paul was not opposing the idea that one could earn salvation by obeying the law, because first-century Judaism did not hold that view. Instead, it assumes that Paul's objective was the full inclusion of Gentiles within the people of God. He was therefore opposing the idea promoted in Galatia that the law, and especially its requirement of circumcision, was a sign of Israel's privileged status, a boundary marker between those in and those out of the covenant. By opposing grace to this view of the law, Paul was opposing the idea of a limitation of divine favor to a single ethnic group.[38]

The various proposals raise a number of questions about the way Paul construes grace in these passages. Is it the free gift of grace that is at the center of Paul's thought in Galatians and Romans, a grace that negates any need to earn salvation? Or is it instead the breadth of God's grace that Paul has in mind, a grace that negates any restriction of salvation to those under the law? Perhaps we are wrong to seek for a single answer.[39] Perhaps Paul's thought, like grace itself, overflowed the logical constraints of his argument (Rom 5:20–21). Yet the fact that this distinctive law-grace opposition appears only in Galatians and Romans, letters where the question of the acceptance of Gentiles was paramount, provides strong support for Dunn's contention that the leading edge of Paul's purpose here was "to free both promise and law for a wider range of recipients, freed from the ethnic constraints which he saw to be narrowing the grace of God."[40]

Yet strong objections have been raised against this proposal. Some are based on different readings of key texts, for Paul does not express himself as clearly as we would like, and he does not attempt—or, if he attempts, he does not achieve—the consistency of explication and application that would provide unambiguous access to his thought. There is, however, a deeper concern behind some of the objections. Justification by grace through faith is regarded by many as the heart of the Christian message. If, however, as some have argued, Paul developed this as a "polemical doctrine" in opposition to a specific position on circumcision that was emerging in Galatia, does that mean it was not foundational to his thought?[41] And if it was not foundational, or if it did not mean for Paul what it means for Christians today, does that undermine Christian assurance and confidence?[42] I think not, but this is a matter for theologians to explore. The pastoral and theological concerns of our own time and place must not, however, dictate what we are able to hear Paul saying in his time and place. And in the situation that emerged in Galatia, it seems to me that the radical inclusiveness of grace was at the center of his argument.

It thus seems ironic that Paul, having demolished the law as a barrier that denies Gentiles access to grace *as Gentiles*, then sets up a christological barrier that denies Jews access to grace *as Jews*.[43] It is, as John Barclay notes, a "subtly 'particularist claim to universalism'" that Paul presents in the name of grace, one that "ultimately delegitimize[s] Jews and all other non-Christians who cannot accept that they are simply 'on the way to destruction' (1 Cor. 1:18)?[44] He asks, "Does Paul have anything at all to offer a world that is not only multicultural but also multireligious?" and then provides an answer that is as thoughtful as any I have read. I quote it at length:

I think myself that Paul partially deconstructs his own Christological exclusivism by his pervasive appeal to the grace of God. The foundation of Paul's gospel, and the basis of his relativization of all
cultures, is his radical appreciation of the grace of God which hum-
bles human pride and subverts the theological and cultural edifices
which "flesh" constructs. The justification of the ungodly and the gift
of the Spirit are, for Paul, acts of grace which undermine absolute
commitment to the law (Rom. 4:4–5; Gal. 3:1–5); he himself had
experienced God's grace as calling into question all his previous cultural assurances (Gal. 1:13–16; 1 Cor. 15:8–10). Paul discerns the gracious initiative of God through Israel's history, and its paradoxical
triumph precisely through her unbelief (Romans 9–11), since the
God who has consigned all to disobedience will ultimately have
mercy on all (Rom. 11:32). This radical notion of divine grace, which
Paul uses to destabilize the church at least as much as those outside
it (cf. 1 Corinthians *passim*), could serve both to affirm and to rela-
tivize the Christian tradition itself. The church exists not for its own
sake but to bear witness to the grace of God. Paul himself is ultimately speechless before the mercy of God and cannot find even
Christian language in which to express its significance (Rom.
11:33–36). To this extent, even Pauline theology could be mobilized
to serve a multiculturalism whose religious basis is the affirming and
relativizing grace of God.[45]

Conclusion

Grace was not, for Paul, a static concept. It is reasonable to assume that
before his encounter with Christ he shared the views of first-century
Judaism and thus that he already had a lively sense of God's grace. His
experience of Christ revealed a new locus of grace in the cross, which
altered his understanding of the connection between grace and human
suffering. His assessment of human vulnerability to sin seems also to have
deepened, and with it his understanding of the power of forgiving grace.
The conflict generated by his mission to the Gentiles opened his eyes to
the radical inclusiveness of grace. Grace was, it seems, on the growing
edge of his theology. And he presents us with a choice, either to take his
insights as a normative expression of grace, or to follow his lead in probing further its limits.

Chapter Two

Paul and the Jewish Law

No aspect of Paul's thought is as hotly disputed as his view of the law. There are conflicting opinions on the role of the law in the Judaism of Paul's day: within and against what views did he stand? There are debates over terminology: Do all his references to *nomos*—a Greek word with a range of nuances[1]—refer to the Jewish law, the Torah? This question is complicated by the neologisms (new expressions) that Paul created: the *nomos* of Christ (Gal 6:2), the *nomos* of sin and death (Rom 8:2), the *nomos* of faith (Rom 3:27), the *nomos* of the Spirit of life (Rom 8:2). Do these evocative phrases also refer—somehow—to the same law? If so, what view of the law do they imply?

The most intense arguments—because they touch foundational issues of revelation and inspiration—concern the consistency of Paul's view of the law. Did Paul's view of the law derive from his conversion experience and remain constant thereafter?[2] Did it develop—logically, organically—in response to Paul's experiences?[3] More specifically, did it emerge—polemically—out of his conflicts with other missionaries?[4] More radical still, did he even have a clear and consistent position on the law, or do the letters reflect ad hoc formulations created to meet various needs?[5]

Upon one issue there is agreement: Paul understood his apostolic call to be a commission to bring a *law-free* gospel to the Gentiles. Their acceptability to God and their membership in the people of God did not depend on their adherence to the Jewish law. These Gentiles were being incorporated into a messianic sect of Judaism. They became children of Abraham (Gal 3:6–7; Rom 4:11–12), heirs of the blessing promised to Abraham's offspring (Gal 3:29; Rom 4:16), grafted onto the root of Israel (Rom 11:17). But they did not have to become Jews![6] That is, they did not have to be circumcised, and they did not have to follow the law. This message required some explanation and defense, especially when Paul's views were challenged by other, more orthodox, Jews. We can make some progress toward contextualizing Paul's view of the law by focusing first on his comments on circumcision, for that initiation rite marked the traditional boundary between those outside the law and those under it.[7]

Circumcision

Though circumcision was practiced by a number of other ethnic groups, most notably in Paul's time by the Egyptians, it was widely regarded as the defining characteristic of the Jew. For male Jews, removal of the foreskin was a necessary physical sign of membership in the covenant people (Gen 17:9–14) and commitment to the covenant law. That was certainly a dominant view in Judaism, but there is evidence that it was not the only view. Around the margins, and especially in the Diaspora, some Jews seem to have held a different view: physical circumcision was *not* an absolute requirement and identity marker for male Jews.[8]

The clearest evidence for this comes from Philo, a first-century CE Jewish philosopher from Alexandria. He defends the practice of circumcision against the ridicule of outsiders, but in doing so he does not mention its importance for Jewish ethnic and religious identity. Quite the contrary, his first point is that circumcision is practiced by other nations as well. He also defends circumcision on hygienic grounds and adds that it serves as a valuable symbol of moral purity, specifically, a symbol of the excision of hedonism and pride (*Spec.* 1.1–11). He notes that some adhere only to this symbolic or "inner" meaning and neglect the physical, "external" rite (*Migr.* 86–93). Such men he rebukes, but he does not deny them the name "Jew." Indeed, Philo himself elsewhere defines the proselyte, the Gentile convert to Judaism, as "one who has circumcised not his uncircumcision but his desires and sensual pleasures and other passions of the soul" (*QE* 2.2). [9] From what he has said elsewhere, it is clear that Philo expected the male proselyte to become physically circumcised, but—in agreement with the "symbolists" mentioned above—it is inner circumcision that, in his view, makes one a Jew.

There is evidence—usually in the form of complaints by traditionalists—that uncircumcised Jews existed in other times and places. *Jubilees* (2nd century BCE) warns against "children of Israel . . . [who] will not circumcise their children according to the law" (15:33–34). First Maccabees describes (and denounces) adult Jews who remove their marks of circumcision (1:15), though it is clear that they continued to regard themselves as Jews.[10] Josephus insists that circumcision is the definitive mark of the Jew, yet he also reports that in at least one exceptional case a proselyte was not required to undergo the rite (*Ant.* 20.2.3–4 §§41–46). The later rabbinic tradition overwhelmingly affirms the requirement of circumcision, yet even within that tradition there was room for debate:

> Our Rabbis taught: If a proselyte was circumcised but did not immerse (in the ritual bath), Rabbi Eliezer says that indeed this is a (valid) proselyte. . . . If he (the proselyte) immersed but was not circumcised, Rabbi Joshua says that indeed this is a (valid) proselyte. . . . But the sages say: If he (the proselyte) immersed but was not circumcised, (or) was circumcised but did not immerse, he is not a (valid) proselyte until he is circumcised and immerses. (*b. Yeb.* 46a)[11]

The point of this survey is to suggest that when Paul treats physical circumcision as an indifferent matter (1 Cor 7:19; Gal 5:6; 6:15), when he asserts that circumcision of the heart (that is, moral change) is what matters (Rom 2:25–29), he is taking a position on the margin, but within the wide range of opinions affirmed by Jews of his day. In Galatians, though, Paul also expresses a stronger opinion. Circumcision for Gentile believers is not a matter of indifference or choice: they *must not* submit to it (Gal 5:2). Paul was, of course, pushed to that assertion (perhaps even pushed to that opinion, if it was not implicit in his earlier statements) by rival missionaries who were insisting that Paul's converts complete their conversion with circumcision as a sign of their membership in the covenant people. Paul's violent objections raise the question, What was wrong with Gentile believers agreeing to be circumcised? Paul's answer is clear: that would bring them under the law (Gal 5:3). But what does Paul see as wrong with complementing faith with works of the law? That question raises a very disputed issue.

"Works of the Law"

Paul uses this phrase six times, always in Galatians or Romans and always opposed to faith: "We know that a person is justified not by the works of the law but through faith in Jesus Christ. And we have come to believe in Christ Jesus, so that we might be justified by faith in Christ, and not by doing the works of the law, because no one will be justified by the works of the law" (Gal 2:16; see also Gal 3:2, 5, 10; Rom 3:20, 28). The phrase "works of the law" is not unique to Paul.[12] It is not even particularly prominent in Paul, but exploring what he might have meant by it exposes the riddle of his view of the law.

For many years the prevailing assumption, particularly in Protestant scholarship, was that "works of the law" referred to good works done in order to gain or achieve righteousness before God. The phrase defined Judaism as a religion of works-righteousness, a "legalistic" (or quid pro quo) system in which one attempted to earn salvation by one's own merits.[13] This attempt, whether successful or not, was rejected by Paul (it is argued) because it embodied the sin of self-pride or self-achievement and encouraged a stance of boastful arrogance before God.[14] Such an interpretation seemed indicated by passages like Rom 4:2 ("For if Abraham was justified by works, he has something to boast about, but not before God"; see also Rom 9:30–33; Phil 3:9), yet curiously undermined by other passages like Phil 3:12 ("Work out your own salvation with fear and trembling"; see also Rom 2:9–10; 2 Cor 5:10). A number of scholars also pointed out that this interpretation did not correspond to what was known of the Judaism of Paul's day,[15] a warning that went largely unheeded until the publication of *Paul and Palestinian Judaism* by E. P. Sanders.[16]

Sanders scoured the writings of Palestinian Judaism from 200 BCE to 200 CE to uncover what he called the "patterns of religion" reflected there. By "pattern of religion" he meant the way a religion was "perceived by its adherents to *function*": how people got in and stayed in on a day-to-day basis.[17] What he found, in spite of significant theological differences in this material, was a common pattern rooted in grace, in which works functioned as a response to God's free election of Israel into covenant relationship. Works were not regarded or performed as a way of achieving merit or salvation. One got into the people of God, he found, purely by grace and lived and remained in the people of God by obedience to the law. Moreover, obedience itself was sustained by grace: the grace of a forgiving God and a divinely instituted means of atonement. Because the law (Greek *nomos*) functioned to regulate life within a covenant of grace, Sanders named this pattern "covenantal nomism."[18]

Sanders's discovery rocked the prevailing consensus about the legalistic interpretation of "works of the law," and various alternatives have subsequently been proposed. Some dispute the accuracy of Sanders's research and interpret first-century Judaism as a variegated but in many ways still legalistic entity.[19] Others accept the accuracy of his description but argue that Paul misunderstood or (more sinisterly) misrepresented the Judaism of his day as legalistic.[20] Sanders himself agreed that Paul was not concerned with accurately representing Judaism on its own terms, but, he said, the reason for this was that God had changed the operative pattern of religion. Paul opposed "works of the law," not because they were inherently flawed, but simply because they were not faith. As Sanders memorably concluded, "What Paul finds wrong in Judaism: it is not Christianity."[21]

The radical discontinuity between Paul and Judaism that Sanders proposed, not to mention his disconcerting proposal of a deity who simply changed the rules, was not, however, widely embraced even by those who accepted his description of Palestinian Judaism. A more satisfying solution—for some, at least—was found by turning once again to the writings of Second Temple Judaism in order to gain a better understanding of the *social* function of the law. James D. G. Dunn, acting on clues found in Sanders's work, pioneered this round of research.[22]

Judaism, Dunn agreed, never regarded the law as a means of earning God's favor. However, the Jewish view of the law did evolve from God's requirement for living within the covenant (an intramural concern) to an expression of Israel's distinctiveness as people of the covenant (an intermural concern). Works of the law, especially circumcision and the food and Sabbath laws, functioned as "identity markers" of God's people, as "badges" of membership, and thus as a "boundary" between God's people and the surrounding nations. In such a role the law also became a mark of the privileged status of God's chosen people. The "works of the law" to which Paul objects, Dunn argues, are works understood in this way as identity badges that mark off one privileged group: "For we hold that a person is justified by faith apart from works prescribed by the law. Or is God the God of Jews only? Is he not the God of Gentiles also?" (Rom 3:29–30).

This "new perspective" on Paul has been embraced by many for the clarity it brings to numerous Pauline texts and the ease with which it fits Paul's social and cultural contexts.[23] It has also been expanded. Tatha Wiley notes that "works of the law" do not mark off *all* Jews as privileged, only *male* Jews. Only men bear the gender-specific mark of the covenant and only their status in homes and in assemblies is enhanced by the covenant law. Paul's resistance to works of the law, she argues, was fueled at least in part by his determination to retain the equality not only of Gentiles and Jews but also of men and women within the body of Christ.[24]

The response to the new perspective has not, however, been universally positive. Some Pauline texts seem resistant to the new perspective, seem, indeed, to yield more naturally to the old perspective (Rom 4:1–5;

Gal 3:10–14). Additionally, some object that, like the earlier interpretation, this one also presents a distorted portrait of Judaism. If a major objection to the old perspective was its depiction of Judaism as a soulless, legalistic religion, the new one provides no real improvement, for it caricatures Judaism as a racist, nationalistic religion.[25] Thus energetic defenses of the old perspective continue to be developed, with varying degrees of accommodation to the insights of the new.

The argument persists that Judaism was indeed legalistic,[26] or that a legalistic form of Judaism existed alongside one defined by covenantal nomism, and that it was against the former, not the latter, that Paul polemicized.[27] Charles Talbert argues that covenantal nomism became, in an eschatological context (that is, when end-time salvation was sharply in view), a legalistic religion. "One may be a part of God's people by grace, but in order to stay in the people and in order to enter into the Age to Come, one must obey the Law. Obedience is the condition for eschatological salvation."[28] It is this eschatological, legalistic form of covenantal nomism (labeled "synergism"), Talbert claims, that is the target of Paul's attack.

In partial deference to the picture of Judaism that emerged from Sanders's investigation, some who retain the legalistic interpretation have softened the contours of Jewish legalism. The effort to obey God's laws, it is argued, need not always entail a self-seeking attitude and the view that one is earning salvation. Works of the law can be performed simply because God has commanded them.[29] On this view Paul rejects "works of the law" not because they reflect human hubris (the attempt to establish a claim on God), or because they restrict God's grace to a single group, but because apart from Christ they cannot be accomplished in a way that meets God's approval.[30] All of these explanations, though presenting a more carefully nuanced version of the old perspective on "works of the law," fail to account for the central roles of divine mercy, forgiveness, and atonement in first-century Judaism.

Other responses to Dunn reject the link with Judaism altogether. The key to this line of interpretation are the addressees of Paul's letters: *Gentile* congregations. When Paul writes to *them* about "works of the law," it is argued, he is not critiquing Jewish observance of the law. Rather, he is warning against "the adoption of selected Jewish practices *on the part of Gentiles.*" *Gentiles* do not need "works of the law," for *they* will be made righteous through Christ.[31] The problem of the Jews is not that they cling to the law instead of believing in Christ, but that they fail to accept that Christ is the goal of the law *for Gentiles.* Those exploring this line of interpretation have produced readings of Paul that are startlingly fresh and provocative, but they are also difficult, for they require abandoning presuppositions that have controlled the reading of Paul for well over fifteen hundred years. Many find it hard to reconcile this interpretation with passages where Paul seems to include Jews in his critique of works of the law (Rom 3:20; 9:30–10:3).[32]

We are left, then, with an apparent stalemate. Legalistic (soft or hard) interpretations of Paul's criticism of "works of the law" fail to do justice to the realities of Second Temple Judaism or to the thrust of Paul's argument in several crucial passages. The new perspective, on the other hand, requires strained exegesis of some other crucial passages. The problem is that trying to fit all of Paul's references to "works of the law" into a single theological framework seems to require strained exegesis at some point. A better approach may be to assume that Paul was flexible in the way he used the phrase. It is likely that Paul did not start his theological reflections on the law by dispassionately analyzing its role in Judaism and then working his way toward God's solution. Rather, as Sanders has insisted, Paul began with his sudden apprehension of the solution and from that perspective worked his way back to the plight.[33] Moreover, the presenting needs of his argument at different points in his different letters dictated his emphasis more than a desire to present objectively the complex reality of first-century Judaism.

Because of the mission context of Paul's letters, the role of "works of the law" in excluding Gentiles from salvation seems to be his primary concern, and it is instructive that the first references to the phrase in Galatians and Romans have this emphasis (Gal 2:11–21; Rom 3:20–31). But in developing his arguments for the inclusion of Gentiles he could (and did) also emphasize the more generic point that works are contravened by grace (Gal 3:21; Rom 4:2–5) yet obedience is enabled by the Spirit (Rom 8:2–4).[34] Whether in his mind this was relevant only for Gentiles is the topic of chapter 6.

The Law: Its Nature and Function

In addition to his specific remarks about works of the law, Paul also comments on the law itself: its origin, nature, and function. It is difficult, however, to extract a "theology of the law" from these comments because they are so varied, so rhetorically charged, and so situation dependent.[35] They are also clustered in only two letters: Galatians and Romans. Paul rarely mentions the law in his other letters. In 1 Corinthians, apart from scattered references to "what is written in the law," there is only one substantive comment (15:56), which is so incongruous in its context that many take it to be a later interpolation. There is a lengthy contrast of the letter and the Spirit in 2 Corinthians 3, but law (*nomos*) is not explicitly mentioned, and the actual point of that discussion is the way Paul's opponents were conducting their mission, not the law per se. Paul contrasts righteousness from the law and righteousness based on faith in Phil 3:9, but there is no sustained discussion. And that is it. On the other hand, the law dominates Romans and Galatians, where the word *nomos* appears 74 and 31 times, respectively. We need, obviously, to focus there, but it is best to begin with separate and purely descriptive accounts. Paul has different things to say about the law in these two letters, and harmonizing them creates problems.

Paul wrote Galatians in the highly charged situation of a battle with other rival missionaries for the hearts and minds of his Gentile Galatian converts. In this context he describes the situation with apocalyptic starkness: believers are part of the new creation (6:14), and the law is irredeemably part of the old.[36] Paul does not deny the law's divine origin, but he does not stress it either. God, he said, issued the irrevocable promise to Abraham (the promise of blessings to Gentiles through the messianic "seed," 3:18); the law, however, was "added" later (3:19). By using the passive voice Paul avoids naming the one who added it. He does say that it was "ordained through angels by a mediator," which suggests heavenly origin;[37] but Paul uses this assertion to dissociate the law from God: "Now a mediator involves more than one party; but God is one" (3:20).[38]

Moreover, Paul equates being under law (3:23) to being under sin (3:22), under a yoke of slavery (5:1), and in prison (3:23). He even equates the Galatians' desire to be under the law with a return to their previous idolatry: "Now, however, that you have come to know God, or rather to be known by God, how can you turn back again [by submitting to circumcision] to the weak and beggarly elemental spirits? How can you want to be enslaved to them *again*?" (4:9). The law, too, he thus suggests, is basically "weak and beggarly" even though it exercises the power of a slave master or prison warden over those "under" it.

Paul assumes, without argument, that the law had a function—now annulled in Christ—of separating Jew from Gentile (2:14–15). He also assumes without argument that it defines the standard of righteous obedience and thus pronounces a curse—overcome in Christ—on those who (inevitably) fail to meet it (3:10–14).[39] The law, he insists, could not and did not have the function of justifying, of making righteous (2:21; 3:11). It had the more limited, temporary, but nevertheless important role of the *paidagōgos*, the slave charged with training, disciplining, and protecting the master's sons until they came of age (3:23–26). Stated somewhat more simply, the law "was added because of [to deal with] transgressions, until the [messianic] offspring should come" (3:19). In *that* sense he can assert that the law was not *against* the promises of God (3:21), though it was clearly not a part of them.

Paul wrote Romans in a situation less polemically charged. He had never been to Rome, and there were no rival missionaries to combat. It is possible, though, that word about his very negative views on the law had reached the Roman churches and upset them, for he seems concerned in this letter to present a more balanced and nuanced argument about the law.[40] Here he attributes the origin of the law unambiguously to God ("the law of God," 7:22, 25) and declares it to be holy, just, good, and spiritual (7:12, 14). This ringing affirmation of the law comes, however, hard on the heels of, and as a correction to, his statements earlier in the letter that link the law tightly to sin and death, to captivity and slavery (5:12–21, esp. v. 20; 7:1–6). Paul has spoken of the law as if it were a power or a controlling force from which one can escape only through death (7:6; cf. 6:7, 12–14). Now he argues that it is a *weak* power, intended for good (7:10, 13) but commandeered by the stronger power of sin and used by that superior power for evil purposes and with tragic results (7:7–25).

Overall in Romans, Paul assesses the intended function of the law more positively. It separates Jews from Gentiles, but not in a way that impugns God's impartiality or disadvantages the Gentiles, for while the Gentiles do not possess the Jewish law, they have its requirements written on their hearts (2:12–16, 25–29; 3:9). The law defines sin (3:20), reveals sin (7:13), "reckons" or keeps count of sin (5:13), and in that sense multiplies sin (5:20). Paul nevertheless asserts greater continuity in this letter between the law and faith than he did in Galatians. Though the saving righteousness of God is now revealed on the basis of faith and apart from law, still the law and the prophets bear witness to it (3:21). And, Paul insists, faith does not overthrow the law (3:31), a remarkable claim that he defends by demonstrating that Abraham's faithfulness and trust were confirmed by circumcision (4:1-12). Indeed, he says, "Christ is the end of the law" (10:4), an ambiguous statement that probably means that Christ is the *goal*, not the termination, of the law.[41]

As in Galatians, Paul insists that believers are no longer under law (Rom 6:14–15), that they have died to the law (7:4). Yet in this letter Paul springs a surprise only hinted at in Galatians:[42] "For God has done what the law, weakened by the flesh, could not do: by sending his own Son in the likeness of sinful flesh, and to deal with sin, he condemned sin in the flesh, *so that the just requirement of the law might be fulfilled in us, who walk not according to the flesh but according to the Spirit*" (8:3–4). This surprising claim that the requirement of the law remains in effect needs careful attention. The Greek word translated "just requirement" (*dikaiōma*) is singular, and so the emphasis is on fulfilling the law's essential demand for righteousness, not on satisfying each of its individual requirements. More significantly, Paul says this essential demand will be fulfilled *in* us; he does not say "by us." In fact, he says it will be fulfilled in us through the indwelling presence of the Holy Spirit,[43] which enables the one possessing that Spirit to live in accordance with God's will by providing the guidance and the power to do so (8:5–11).

This resolves a final puzzle of the law. Paul indicates in several places that in some way the law will be the standard of judgment for everyone, even for those who are not "under" it (Rom 2:12–16; 13:9; Gal 5:14). It is now clear that this is so because the law's function as an expression of God's righteous will does not change. Those who are led and empowered by the Spirit will fulfill this righteous will even though they might never consult or deliberately obey the commandments of Moses. It is probably in this light that the striking phrases "the law of faith" (Rom 3:27), "the law of the Spirit of life" (Rom 8:2), even "the law of Christ" (Gal 6:2) are to be understood. Though the issue is disputed,[44] they probably refer to the law as fulfilled by active and obedient faith (Rom 1:5; 16:26), the law's righteousness as fulfilled by those who walk in the Spirit, or the law's righteous requirement fulfilled—specifically through the love command—by those in Christ.

What emerges here, as several have noticed, is something that looks very much like the covenantal nomism that, according to Sanders, defined Palestinian Judaism:[45] (1) God's gracious initiative in establishing a relationship: in Judaism, in the giving of the covenant; here, in the sending of Christ; (2) the human response that maintains the relationship: in Judaism, life in obedience to the covenant; here, life in Christ, which is life in the Spirit, which is life in accord with the righteousness the law describes; (3) final judgment.

Conclusion

Interpretations of Paul's statements on the law, especially his rejection of "works of the law," seem driven to a large extent by extratextual concerns about consistency, about preserving the truth of Christianity as the interpreter conceives it, about anti-Semitic (more correctly, anti-Jewish) consequences. The debate can be advanced only by careful exegesis of Paul's often convoluted and ambiguous Greek, a task that lies far beyond the limitations of this essay. Suffice it to say that one's understanding of the dynamics of Paul's argument is strongly affected by exegetical decisions about certain key texts (e.g., Gal 2:16 or Rom 10:4) and by the way one construes the contrasting element—*pistis*, "faith" or "trust," *Iēsou Christou*, "of" or "in Jesus Christ." Currently there is no consensus and no evidence that one is emerging. Some matters, though, are reasonably clear.

Paul's zealous concern about the law evinced in Romans and Galatians did not begin with his conversion. By his own admission, his persecution of the followers of Christ was also rooted in his zeal "for the traditions of my ancestors," that is, his zeal for the law, presumably because these traditions, this law, were being undermined by the new messianic sect.[46] Paul emerged from his encounter with Christ equally zealous for his new commission: to bring the good news of salvation to Gentiles. Faith was all that was necessary, and faith was alone sufficient. They did not need to come under the law.

For Jews, those who were the object of the mission work of Peter and James and John (Gal 2:8–9), there seems to have been no objection to their continuing obedience to the law as a complement to their faith. This makes Paul's absolute opposition to it for Gentiles seem faintly irrational, as his opponents doubtless argued, especially when he reintroduced fulfillment of the law as the goal of the Spirit-led life. But Paul's response was dictated by his opponents' insistence that Gentile believers were *required* to come under the law, that is, to become Jews, in order to be full members of God's people. To Paul that meant that Gentiles *as Gentiles* were not acceptable to God, yet the workings of the Spirit among the men and women in Galatia provided compelling evidence, to Paul at least, that Gentiles *were* acceptable—as Gentiles—to God. Therefore Gentiles must not come "under law"—that is, become Jews—for to do so would deny the reality of the grace they had all experienced. Paul's opposition to Gentiles coming "under law" did not, however, mean that Paul condoned lawless behavior. The Spirit, he insisted, was a reliable guide to God's righteous will and a powerful enabler of obedience to it.

Chapter Three

Faith

For Paul, *pistis*, usually translated "faith," was the essential characteristic of those he called, appropriately enough, "believers."[1] He used
other words and phrases to describe them as well: they were "saints" or
"holy ones," "beloved," and "called" or "chosen ones" (see, e.g., Rom
1:7). They were (or should have been) characterized by love, righteousness, hope, peace, and endurance. But when Paul reported what was proclaimed abroad about them (1 Thess 1:8), what he most feared their
losing (1 Thess 3:5), what he most celebrated their having (1 Thess 3:7–9),
it was to their *pistis*, their faith, that he referred. In a fundamental way *pistis* defined them in their relationship to God.[2] The same thing, however,
was true of many strands of contemporary Judaism. In 4 Maccabees, in
Sirach, and especially in the writings of Philo, *pistis* appears as a central
feature of Jewish self-definition.[3] Several things, however, distinguished
Paul's use of the term from that of Greek-speaking Jewish writers: he
opposed *pistis* to the Jewish law instead of coordinating it with obedience
to the law, he related *pistis* to Christ, and he emphasized not only the element of trust that predominates in Jewish uses of the term, but also—and
some say especially—an element of assent to (that is, belief in) the content of the gospel. The last point suggests that before exploring how Paul
understood *pistis* to be related to Christ and to the law, we must establish
the basic meaning of the word.

The Meaning(s) of *Pistis/Pisteuein*

The noun *pistis* and the verb *pisteuein*, formed in Greek from the same root
(*pist**), are usually rendered in English with words formed from different

stems: "faith" (from Latin *fides*) for the noun, and "believe" (from Middle English *bileven*) for the verb. Both in dictionaries and in general usage, "faith" has the primary meaning of belief in the truth of something, even, or especially, in the absence of material evidence. Likewise, "believe" has the primary meaning of accepting something as true or real.[4] Neither of these two English words, however, conveys all the shades of meaning found in the Greek terms. The primary nuance of the Greek noun, for example, is trust or confidence (highlighting an active stance of firm reliance on someone or something). It can also suggest, as the English does, credence or belief (emphasizing the intellectual activity of assent to the truth of something or the truthfulness of someone); it can imply faithfulness or trustworthiness (focusing on the moral steadfastness of one's deeds and words); and it can designate the proof or evidence upon which confidence or belief can be based. Likewise, the nuances of the verb range from trusting in something (or someone), relying on something (or someone), to believing that something is true, with various prepositions or conjunctions ("in," "on," or "that") often used to clarify the nature and object of the activity.

Paul's use of these words covers this whole range of meanings. He sometimes specifies content (*what* is believed), emphasizing the element of intellectual assent ("believe in your heart *that* God raised him from the dead," Rom 10:9; see also 1 Thess 4:14). Other times he stresses the moral aspect by linking the word with references to obedience ("to bring about the obedience of faith among all the Gentiles," Rom 1:5; also 16:26; see also 10:16), and he promotes the nuance of trust through the example of Abraham (Rom 4:16–22).[5] Some have argued that one of these aspects is more foundational for Paul than the others, but there is no agreement over which has that status.[6] It is more important to view the various nuances as a continuum than to resolve their absolute ranking. Trust in God (or Christ) is necessarily rooted in the belief that what is said about God (or Christ) is true, whether it be promise or proclamation. And real trust necessarily manifests itself in the way one lives one's life, that is, in actions. Paul promotes different aspects of *pistis* at different points in his arguments, but the full range of nuances is always at least potentially present. Central, though, to the importance of the concept for Paul, and regardless of which aspect is in view, is the conviction, expressed in a variety of ways, that *pistis* is the appropriate and saving response to the gospel: "Therefore *pistis* is from hearing, and hearing is through the word about Christ" (Rom 10:17 AT; see Rom 10:5–17; 1 Cor 15:1–2; 1 Thess 1:2–8).

Faith versus the Law

In several of his letters, most notably Galatians and Romans, Paul sharpens the meaning of *pistis* by contrasting it with another way of relating to God—through works of the (Jewish) law. In Hellenistic-Jewish writings these were seen as complementary actions. Philo, a first-century CE Jew of Alexandria, describes *pistis* as "the most perfect of virtues" (*Her.* 91). As with Paul, this virtue is closely associated with Abraham, and the element of trust dominates its meaning. Abraham, according to Philo, believed (and trusted) the promises of God, specifically the promise that he would inherit wisdom (*Her.* 101).[7] Significantly, however, after extensive praise of Abraham's *pistis*, Philo notes as the "crowning" comment "that this man did the divine law and the divine commands" (*Abr.* 275). *Pistis* and obedience to the law are aligned, not opposed, in Philo's writings.

Likewise, 4 Maccabees, written in the Hellenistic-Jewish Diaspora between the first century BCE and the second century CE, notes that the Jews who were tortured and killed by Antiochus IV Epiphanes (2nd century BCE) accepted their death with great courage because of their *pistis*. This *pistis* embraced both their utter trust in God and their belief that they, like Abraham, Isaac, and Jacob, would "live to God," that is, be with God after their death (7:16–23; cf. 16:22). Significantly, their trust was demonstrated precisely by their loyalty to the law: "Let us with all our hearts consecrate ourselves to God, who gave us our lives, and let us use our bodies as a bulwark for the law" (13:13). Finally, Sirach,[8] written in the second century BCE, identifies through poetic parallelism those who trust (*pisteuein*) in God as precisely those who keep God's law:

> The one who keeps the law
>   preserves himself,
> and the one who trusts the Lord
>   will not suffer loss.
>   (32:24; see also 2:7–17)

For all these writers, trust in God and obedience to God's law were but two sides of the same coin. Paul, however, presents the two as antithetical: "Yet we know that a person is justified not by the works of the law but through faith in Jesus Christ. And we have come to believe in Christ Jesus, so that we might be justified by faith in Christ, and not by doing the works of the law, because no one will be justified by the works of the law" (Gal 2:16).[9] Clearly this antithesis has implications for Paul's view of the nature and significance of faith, but what these implications are is hotly contested. Much depends on how one interprets Paul's opposition to works of the law.

The prevailing interpretation of Paul's objection to works of the law is that works represent "works-righteousness," the attempt to achieve or "earn" salvation on one's own merits. Such an attempt is seen as not only misguided, inasmuch as achieving salvation remains beyond the reach of sinful humanity, but also (in some interpretations) sinful, inasmuch as the very attempt to earn salvation is an attempt to "put God in one's debt."[10] This, it is argued, constitutes a denial of one's "dependence upon God the Creator," and this denial is the essence of sin.[11] Faith, in this context and according to this interpretation, is the antithesis of achievement. It is an act of obedience and surrender, "the radical opposite of the attitude of 'boasting'" engendered by works.[12] Although it is a "free deed of decision,"[13] it is not an accomplishment. Yet—and here is the problem—it *seems* like an accomplishment. When Bultmann states that "'faith' is the condition for the receipt of 'righteousness,' taking the place of 'works,'"[14] one could conclude that the basic formula remains the same: a person is justified by the adequacy of one's faith instead of by the adequacy of one's deeds. "Faith" *seems* to be a type of "work."

Bultmann argues vigorously against this conclusion, yet he does so primarily by defining faith as not an accomplishment. It is, he says, "the radical renunciation of accomplishment."[15] Cranfield agrees: "[Faith] is not a contribution from [the human] side which, by fulfilling a condition laid down by God, enables the gospel to be saving. In that case," he admits, "faith would be, in the last resort, a meritorious work." But, says Cranfield, "it is of the very essence of faith, as Paul understands it, that it is opposed to all human deserving, all human establishing of claims on God."[16] Now Paul himself does not explicitly define faith in this way, so how do Cranfield, Bultmann, and others following this line of interpretation know that it is so? Because they understand "works of the law" as an attempt to establish a claim on God, and Paul sets faith opposed to this. But what if that understanding of "works of the law" is incorrect?

James D. G. Dunn argues that it *is* incorrect. The problem of the law, he says, is not that it promotes works-righteousness. It does no such thing.[17] Rather, Paul objects to "the law misunderstood by a misplaced emphasis on boundary-marking ritual," in which works function to divide Jew from non-Jew, to distinguish those within the covenant from those without.[18] In *this* context the emphasis Paul intends by contrasting faith with works is that "God's saving act is for *all* who believe, *without dis-*

tinction" (Rom 3:22), that is, without privileging those with the physical marks of the covenant.[19] According to this view, it is of the very essence of *pistis* that it is an *impartial* means of appropriating God's gift, one that all can exercise. Faith stands opposed, then, not to human merit and boasting but to "Jewish national self-confidence based on their being the people of the law."[20]

Dunn's proposal draws Paul closer to Judaism insofar as *pistis* and the law (properly understood without an emphasis on boundaries) can once again be coordinated (Rom 3:31).[21] Yet a substantial difference remains. For Paul, *pistis* is related to Christ. But how is it related?

Faith in Christ or Faith of Christ?

When Paul specifies the object of the activity of believing or trusting, he usually mentions God (Rom 4:3, 5, 17, 24; Gal 3:6; 1 Thess 1:8).[22] For Paul, as for Judaism, faith is inherently theocentric.[23] It is God whom one obeys (Rom 6:13, 22), God in whom one trusts (Rom 4:5),[24] and God's acts and promises that one believes (Rom 10:9). Yet for Paul faith and trust are directed specifically toward God's offer of salvation through the death and resurrection of Jesus Christ, and in that sense it is also faith in Christ.[25] That is, it is the belief that God's offer of salvation through Christ is true and that Christ is now Lord, and it is utter trust in and obedience to the one who has offered that salvation and made him Lord.[26]

There are, however, several passages in Paul's undisputed letters that speak, or seem to speak, of Christ's own faith or faithfulness (Rom 3:22, 26; Gal 2:16 [twice], 20; 3:22; Phil 3:9; see also Eph 3:12). If that is the correct interpretation, the relationship between the believer's faith and Christ acquires additional complexity. But the issue is hotly debated. At the heart of the question is an ambiguous Greek phrase that can be translated either "faith of Christ" or "faith in Christ." English translations have consistently chosen the latter; indeed, one has to go back to the King James Bible (1611) to find a major translation that presents the alternative. Yet the arguments for the "of Christ" translation are much stronger than the history of English translations would indicate, and support for this alternative is growing.[27] The arguments are technical and somewhat tedious, but necessary to grasp if one is interested in evaluating the alternatives.

The Greek phrase consists of the noun "faith" (*pistis*) followed by Jesus' name or title (Jesus, Christ, Jesus Christ, or Son of God) in the genitive case (e.g., *pistis Christou*). In Greek this case can mark, among other things, the *object* of the action indicated by the preceding noun (here, *pistis* that has Christ as its object; hence, faith in Christ), or the *subject*—that is, the doer[28]—of the action of the preceding noun (here, *pistis* that Christ himself exhibits; hence, faith of Christ). The former is referred to in grammar books as the "objective genitive," the latter as the "subjective genitive." A similar ambiguity can be found in the English phrase "love of God," which can refer to love for God (objective genitive) or God's love (for others) (subjective genitive). Nothing in this phrase alone, or in the *pistis* phrase in question, encourages one reading over another. Other factors—contextual, exegetical, and theological—are employed to decide on or to defend a particular interpretation. What factors, then, support or oppose the different options regarding *pistis*?[29]

The translation "faith in Christ" is, first, strongly supported by tradition, especially since the sixteenth century.[30] As noted above, this translation has been consistently favored in English translations. Earlier translations into Coptic, Syriac, and Latin are more ambiguous.[31] Second, the fact that Paul refers to believing or trusting in Christ using other, less ambiguous, grammatical constructions (e.g., the verb *pisteuein*, "to believe," with the preposition *eis*, "in," or *epi*, "on") leads some to conclude that he intended the more ambiguous phrase (*pistis* + genitive) to be understood in the same way. Third, with a single exception (Eph 3:12), the ambiguous phrase is not found in the deutero-Pauline letters (letters attributed to Paul but probably written by followers of Paul). These letters contain instead unambiguous references to "faith in Christ": the noun *pistis* with the preposition *en*, "in" (e.g., Eph 1:15; Col 1:4; 1 Tim 3:13; 2 Tim 1:13; 3:15).[32] There are, however, two ways of interpreting this evidence. It could be an indication that some of Paul's earliest followers clarified his original intent by using a less ambiguous phrase. On the other hand, it could indicate that different phrases were used by Paul and his followers to refer to different things: the faith of Christ (*pistis* + genitive) and faith in Christ (*pistis* with the preposition).[33] Finally, supporters of "faith in Christ" ask why, if the faith of Christ were so important, did Paul not describe in more detail how Christ displayed this faith? Apart from this phrase, there are no clear references to Christ's faith in Paul's letters. Supporters of "faith of Christ" respond that Paul can describe Jesus' faithful actions without necessarily using the word *pistis*. Noting that elsewhere Paul equates *pistis* and obedience (e.g., Rom 1:5; 10:16), they claim that in speaking of Jesus' obedience, especially in accepting his death (Rom 5:18–19 and Phil 2:6–8), Paul is speaking of Jesus' *pistis*.[34]

The translation "faith of Christ" is strongly supported, first, by the *general* use of the noun *pistis* followed by a personal noun or pronoun in the genitive case. This construction appears only rarely in the writings of Hellenistic Judaism, but when it does appear it is almost exclusively as a subjective ("faith of") genitive.[35] That Paul tacitly assumes that the Romans (who have not heard him teach or preach or explain this phrase) will understand it argues, some claim, in favor of interpreting it in terms of this customary usage.[36] Second, in addition to the seven instances where Paul follows *pistis* with a reference to Christ, he uses the construction twenty-four times with a different referent. In all of these the reference is to the faith or trust or faithfulness *of* the individual, that is, the subjective genitive.[37] Against this compelling background, Hays argues, "'Faith *in* Jesus Christ' is not the most natural translation of *pistis Christou*."[38] Third, in particular, the ambiguous genitive phrases in Romans that *may* refer to the faith of Christ (3:22, 26) are surrounded by passages that use precisely parallel phrases (*pistis* + genitive) and clearly refer to the faithfulness *of* God (3:3) and the faith *of* Abraham (4:12, 16). In this context, some argue, a reader inclined toward consistency would be strongly encouraged to read the phrase as "faith of Christ."[39]

Proponents of the "faith of Christ" reading acknowledge that Paul speaks clearly of believing in Christ, and they admit that the ambiguous phrase *pistis Christou* is closely integrated into passages that contain these clear statements. But, in their view, that very integration generates support for the reading they prefer. If *pistis Christou* is translated "faith in Christ," the result, they claim, is an awkward and wooden redundancy, which is easily relieved by translating the phrase as a subjective genitive:

> Yet we know that a person is justified not by the works of the law but *through faith in Jesus Christ*. And we have come to *believe in Christ Jesus*, so that we might be justified *by faith in Christ*, and not by doing the works of the law. (Gal 2:16 NRSV)

> Yet we know that a person is justified not by the works of the law but through the faithfulness of Jesus Christ. And we have come to believe in [lit. into] Christ Jesus, so that we might be justified by the faithfulness of Christ, and not by works of the law. (Gal 2:16 AT)[40]

But where proponents of the subjective reading ("faith of Christ") see redundancy, those preferring "faith in" see instead a form of emphasis: Paul urges his point by stating it repeatedly and in various formulations.[41]

Different presuppositions about what constitutes unacceptable grammatical awkwardness control this aspect of the debate.

Other arguments rest even more obviously on theological presuppositions. In support of the "faith in Christ" reading, it is claimed

> a. that the "faith of Christ" option undermines the Reformation emphasis on (human) faith alone;
> b. that faith is inappropriate for the Son of God, who is more appropriately the object of faith; [42]
> c. that the natural contrast to human *works* is human *faith* in Christ.[43]

In support of the "faith of Christ" reading, it is claimed

> a. that with the "faith in Christ" option, justification rests entirely on human believing, which risks turning faith into a "bizarre sort of work";[44]
> b. that "faith in Christ" assigns to Jesus an entirely passive role and does not provide a solid christological grounding for ethics;[45]
> c. that the natural contrast to *human* works is *Christ's* faithfulness.[46]

The cogency of these arguments may become clearer if the shape of the "faith of Christ" option is more fully explored. In particular, the relationship between Christ's faith and human faith needs to be explained. Justification, the gift of righteousness, Paul says, comes through faith (Rom 3:21, 28, 30). But whose? And how? The possibility that Christ's own faith plays a role raises these Reformation-era questions anew.

The answer to these questions clearly lies in the claim that somehow Christ's faith, the radical trust and obedience that led him to accept the cross, becomes our own: "It is no longer I who live, but it is Christ who lives in me. And the life I now live in the flesh I live by the faith/fulness of the Son of God who loved me and gave himself for me" (Gal 2:20 AT). Various ways of describing how his faith becomes ours have been offered: (1) *By imitation* of the example of Christ. Explanations favoring this language promote the idea that robust human activity, modeled on Christ's, is necessary and adequate. The words of Sam Williams show this tendency: "Christian faith is Christ-faith, that relationship to God which Christ exemplified."[47] Williams attempts to modify the notion of *mere* imitation, suggesting that Christ "created" this faith, "actualized" it, and made it "available as a real human possibility."[48] And he suggests that there is a "personal union" with Christ that makes this faith possible.[49]

But he does not explain the nature of that union and insists that each individual is responsible for "remembering Christ's exemplary obedience and yielding oneself in total obedience to God, as Christ did."[50] For Williams, the crucial idea here is "likeness."[51] (2) *By identifying* with Christ.[52] This explanation avoids the implication that mere imitation is adequate, but it lacks clarity. What does it mean to "identify" with Christ? (3) *By mystical union* with or *participation in* Christ.[53] This way of describing the relationship between Christ's faith and human faith respects the explicitness of Paul's language of union with Christ (Rom 6:3; 8:1, 10; 2 Cor 5:17; Gal 3:27). It assumes that the believer is actually united with Christ, participating in Christ (or Christ dwelling in her) through a mystical union; and because of that she shares or participates in Christ's faith just as she participates in Christ's death (Rom 6). Christ's faith becomes hers by virtue of her being one with Christ, just as in him she partakes of his righteousness (1 Cor 1:30; 2 Cor 5:21) and wisdom (1 Cor 1:30). Two final aspects of this option need to be addressed: how one comes to be in Christ and the transformative implications of that union.

Morna Hooker raises an interesting question: "Is it a case of believing in him, and so entering into Christ? Or is it rather that, because we are in him, we share his faith?"[54] When the question is posed this way it resembles the chicken-and-egg conundrum: Which comes first? Logically, it would seem, *ours* does: "We cannot share in what Christ *is* until we enter him, and . . . we enter him by believing in him, so that our faith must come first."[55] As Hooker notes, though, the logic of participation is not linear.

Paul describes the process of uniting with Christ in two ways: baptism into Christ (*eis Christon*, Rom 6:3; Gal 3:27) and believing into Christ (*eis Christon*, Rom 10:14; Gal 2:16; Phil 1:29).[56] These two expressions are grammatically parallel; both employ the same preposition (*eis*), one that implies movement, and both seem to function as "transfer terminology."[57] "One *believes* into Christ."[58] What this strange-sounding assertion seems to imply is that one moves into union with Christ through an act of Christlike trust. This act is not, however, mere imitation of Christ's *pistis*; it is an act that claims and receives Christ's saving *pistis* as one's own. On this model Christ's *pistis* and human *pistis*, though initially separate, fuse into one.

Those who are in Christ partake of Christ's *pistis*. Paul does not, however, seem to regard this *pistis* as a garment-like quality that is put on to conceal a reality of less-than-perfect human *pistis*. Hooker points us in the right direction here. There are, she notes, passages in Paul—most notably

Gal 4:19: "My little children, for whom I am again in the pain of child-birth until Christ is formed in you"—suggesting that participation in Christ is a transforming union whereby those in Christ are conformed to Christ as "Christ is formed in them." Those who participate in Christ's faith grow into that faith. As Hooker says, "Those who share in Christ's faith share already in his righteousness; sanctification is indeed a matter of becoming what one is. Christian life is a matter of conformity to Christ from beginning to end—a sharing in what he is: this is the whole matter of justifying faith and sanctifying obedience."[59]

Conclusion

The faith that Paul knows is a robust faith. It involves committed obedience and radical trust as much as it does assent to the truth of claims about God and Christ. As the Letter of James says of a faith that is merely assent: "Even the demons believe—and shudder" (Jas 2:19). Paul's faith is God-directed and Christ-defined. Whether "Christ-defined" means only that Christ defines the means of God's revelation and the vehicle of the salvation that God offers or also includes Christ's own faith is a matter that is vigorously debated. If the latter is correct, it has several interesting and important consequences.

1. It encourages a greater emphasis on the humanness of Jesus—his trust in and faithfulness to God become soteriologically significant.[60]

2. It permits the emphases of the Gospel narratives and of Paul's letters to be more easily reconciled. The tension between the Gospels' emphasis on the life of Jesus and Paul's resolute focus on the crucifixion and resurrection of Jesus (1 Cor 2:2; see also 2 Cor 5:16) is obvious. If, however, the faithfulness Jesus displayed during his life is of theological significance to Paul, that tension is reduced or eliminated. Paul and the Gospels meet, as it were, in Gethsemane.

3. It also facilitates the coordination of two lines of thought in Paul's letters that have long been viewed as jarringly independent: the juridical concept of justification by faith (e.g., Rom 1–4) and the participatory concept of baptism into Christ (e.g., Rom 5–8). If faith involves participation in Christ, the two lines of thought merge into one.

This focused discussion of the importance of faith for the individual who responds—or does not—to the message of salvation, who trusts and obeys God, who participates in Christ, should not obscure the important fact that for Paul and his ministry the significance of faith was more group oriented. Faith, as Paul understood it, facilitated the inclusion of outsiders—Gentiles—into the people of God. Faith can be manifested through obedience to the law (Rom 8:4), but it is not restricted to that and so is open to all. And on one reading of Rom 3:21–22, Christ's faithfulness revealed and fulfilled God's own covenant faithfulness to Israel.[61]

But that is the topic of chapter 5.

Chapter Four

In Christ

Mystical Reality or Mere Metaphor?

In Gal 2:19–20 Paul says, "I have been *crucified with Christ*; and it is no longer I who live, but it is *Christ who lives in me*." In 2 Cor 5:17 he proclaims, "So if anyone is *in Christ*, there is a new creation!" In Rom 6:3 he asks, "Do you not know that all of us who have been *baptized into Christ Jesus* were *baptized into his death*?" In Rom 8:10 he asserts, "But if *Christ is in you*, though the body is dead because of sin, the Spirit is life because of righteousness." And in Gal 3:27 he instructs, "As many of you as were *baptized into Christ* have *clothed yourselves with Christ*."

Over seventy years ago Albert Schweitzer insisted that all these statements (and others like them) refer to a mystical union with Christ and bluntly claimed that "Christ mysticism is the centre of [Paul's] thought."[1] Others, however, have resisted that conclusion: "'To be in the spirit' no more denotes the state of ecstasy than 'to be in Christ' is a formula of mysticism."[2] Where do scholars stand today on this question? Is the language of being in Christ or dying and rising with Christ "merely metaphorical," or does it reflect a "simple reality"?[3] If it is a reality, how does Paul speak of it, and what does he mean by it? And, most important, what are the implications for those "in Christ"?

The Controversy

Like Schweitzer (but a bit earlier and with more florid prose), Adolf Deissmann located the center of Paul's religion in his mystical union with Christ: "Paul in Christ, Christ in Paul! Paul is full of Christ!"[4] All of Paul's more "theological" concepts stream, he says, from this central point.[5] Not everyone, however, was so certain. Generations of scholars were influenced instead by Rudolf Bultmann's contention that the "mystical" language found in Paul's letters was a legacy of the Hellenistic church.[6] Paul, though not entirely free of this way of thinking, employed the language in a different way. "'In Christ,' far from being a formula for mystic union, is primarily an *ecclesiological* formula. It means the state of having been articulated into the 'body of Christ' [i.e., the church] by baptism. . . . It often expresses in a quite general way the state of being determined by Christ whereby it supplies the lack of the not yet coined adjective 'Christian.'"[7] Hans Conzelmann also rejected any mystical content for Paul's "in Christ" statements. They often mean, he says, little more than that salvation is "through" Christ or express "the objective foundation and the inner-worldly intangibility of Christian existence."[8] Günter Bornkamm was clearer and even more emphatic: "expressions [like Gal 3:27; Rom 8:9–10, etc.] have little in common with mysticism, even where their diction approximates to it."[9] According to these scholars, Paul may occasionally *sound* like a mystic, but mysticism was nowhere near the center of Paul's thought.

A decade later J. Christiaan Beker opened his signature work on Paul with a reference to Deissmann, but he did so only to reject Deissmann's conclusion. Paul's conversion may have been a mystical phenomenon, but, says Beker, what is central for Paul's thought is not "personal subjectivism" or an "intra-psychic phenomenon" (Beker's dismissive way of describing Paul's mystical experience), but "the new state of affairs . . . that concerns the nations and the creation";[10] that is, it concerns apocalyptic eschatology. Jürgen Becker exemplifies another response. He does not explicitly reject a mystical element in Paul's thought, but his treatment of "mystical" passages is brief and very bland: "It is clear that through this language Paul wants to emphasize the personal side of the new relationship to God and Christ."[11] Thus in various ways—by reinterpretation, by explicit rejection, and by silence—the importance of a mystical element in Paul's thought was effectively denied.[12]

There were exceptions to this trend, and important ones. Michel Bouttier rejected many of Deissmann's broadest claims but agreed that "in Christ" often meant real inclusion and participation.[13] Denys E. H. Whiteley took Paul's language of participation in Christ very seriously; indeed, he made it the centerpiece of his interpretation of Paul's theory of atonement. Rejecting the more common substitutionary theory, whereby God transfers to Jesus the punishment due to humans on account of their sin, he proposed instead that Paul's understanding "was one of salvation through participation: Christ shared all our experience, sin alone excepted, including death, in order that we, by virtue of our solidarity with him, might share his life."[14] Explaining the meaning of this "solidarity," he commented, "'incorporation' is not too strong a word."[15]

Ernst Käsemann noted the difference between the worldview of Paul and that of his interpreters and insisted "that what seems to us mythological was viewed by Paul quite realistically."[16] Thus he concludes, "It is not meant metaphorically when Paul says that baptism and the eucharist involve us in Jesus' death, incorporate us 'in Christ' and allow us to participate in the divine Spirit."[17] And E. P. Sanders argued vigorously that "the main points of Schweitzer's analysis [are] precisely correct,"[18] to wit, "the realism with which Paul thought of incorporation in the body of Christ, . . . [which is] the heart of his theology."[19]

This view seems to be growing in popularity. There has been a shift in terminology: the language of "mysticism," deemed by many to be confusing or discomfiting,[20] is often replaced by references to "participation" or, less frequently, "interchange." And debate continues, even among those who accept the reality of Paul's language of participation, over what this participation actually entails. Sanders, I think, speaks for many when he asks, "But what does this [language of participation] mean? How are we to understand it? We seem to lack a category of 'reality'—real participation in Christ, real possession of the Spirit—which lies between naïve cosmological speculation and belief in magical transference on the one hand and a revised self-understanding on the other."[21] John Ashton has, I think, put his finger on the problem: "Paul [was] a real mystic" and the issue is "a matter of visionary insight rather than of logical thought."[22] This suggests that only another mystic can grasp the "category of reality" of which Paul speaks, and mystical scholars are few and far between. Yet whatever the language used and whatever the level of insight into the nature of the reality, more and more scholars of a nonmystical bent are acknowledging that some form of *real* union with Christ was important, even central, to Paul's experience and thought.[23]

The Language of Participation

Paul uses a number of phrases that suggest union with Christ. He speaks of Christ being "in" him or "in" those to whom he writes. Reversing the image, he speaks of himself or his readers being "in Christ," being "members of Christ," or being "members of the body of Christ." He indicates transition by speaking of being "baptized into Christ," and, most radically, he refers to being "baptized into Christ's death" and being "crucified with

Christ."[24] Paul often uses different phrases in close conjunction, and sometimes almost interchangeably,[25] so it may be somewhat artificial and misleading to investigate them separately—as if Paul had carefully distinguished among them. Paul's thought and language seem to be very fluid and flexible, but it is nevertheless helpful, at least initially, to focus on the phrases one by one. Not all of these phrases are read as easily or as frequently as expressions of mystic union.

Christ in you/me. Though not the most prevalent or prominent phrase, Paul's claim that Christ is in him or in his readers may be the easiest to unpack, and thus it is a good place to begin. He makes this statement in four passages in three different letters: Gal 1:16; 2:20; Rom 8:10; 2 Cor 13:5 (see also Gal 4:19; Col 1:27, which may have been written by a follower of Paul, also contains the phrase). Of these, Rom 8:9–10 seems to provide the most fruitful insights into Paul's meaning:

> But you are not in the flesh; you are in the Spirit, since the Spirit of God dwells in you. Anyone who does not have the Spirit of Christ does not belong to him. But if Christ is in you, though the body is dead because of sin, the Spirit is life because of righteousness.

In this passage Paul speaks interchangeably of the "Spirit of God," the "Spirit of Christ," and "Christ" dwelling within the believer, and all of these phrases seem to designate the same entity he refers to elsewhere as the "Holy Spirit." Apparently Paul identified the Spirit that they received upon their confession of faith (Gal 3:1–5) and that served as a sign of their new status as children of God (Gal 4:4–6) as the Spirit of the risen Christ. Indeed, he identified the two so closely that it made no difference to him if he spoke of the Spirit of Christ[26] or of Christ himself dwelling within.

I cannot repeat often enough that Paul was not a systematic theologian and did not work out for his readers a consistent way of referring to and relating these entities; but 1 Cor 15:45 suggests one direction of his thought: "Thus it is written, 'The first man, Adam, became a living being'; the last Adam [that is, Christ] became a life-giving spirit." The NRSV does not capitalize the word "spirit" in this verse[27] and thus downplays any link with the Holy Spirit or with Paul's references elsewhere to the Spirit of Christ. Yet, as Dunn notes, there is little difference between "life-giving Spirit" (Greek *pneuma zōopoioun*) here and "Spirit of life" (Greek *pneuma tēs zōēs*) in Rom 8:2 or the statement that "the Spirit gives life" (Greek *to de pneuma zōopoiei*) in 2 Cor 3:6. Since the last two are generally recognized as references to the Holy Spirit, 1 Cor 15:45 is appropriately interpreted to mean that "Christ is experienced in and through, even *as* the life-giving Spirit."[28]

With this identification, the striking assertion that Christ dwells within seems equivalent to the more familiar claim that the Holy Spirit (or the Spirit of or from God) dwells within (e.g., Rom 8:11; 1 Cor 2:12; 3:16; 6:19; 1 Thess 4:8). Language about the indwelling Spirit, however, is not often interpreted as a reference to mystical union; rather, it is generally understood to refer more simply to the divine presence.[29] Yet Paul's comments on the indwelling spirit of Christ move in a distinctly mystical direction:

> Do you not know that whoever is united to a prostitute becomes one body with her? For it is said, "The two shall be one flesh." But anyone united to the Lord becomes one spirit with him. Shun fornication! Every sin that a person commits is outside the body; but the fornicator sins against the body itself. Or do you not know that your body is a temple of the Holy Spirit within you, which you have from God, and that you are not your own? (1 Cor 6:16–19)

The images are fluid as Paul weaves together the ideas of being united to the Lord, becoming one spirit with the Lord, and the body as a temple of the Holy Spirit. Paul's argument seems to presuppose that the Holy Spirit within the body is the Spirit of Christ, which unites with the human spirit so intimately that the two become one spirit, just as two bodies become one in sexual intercourse.[30]

One should note that this way of speaking of a union with Christ would have been readily understood by Paul's original hearers and readers, who lived in a culture that regarded the body as subject to invasion by daimons, deities, angels, spirits, and the like. They understood as well that such "invasions" could result in a union with the daimon that altered the very being of a person.[31] Paul's message about becoming one spirit with the indwelling Lord was of a piece with their own cultural views.

In Christ (members of Christ, members of the body of Christ).[32] Just as Paul can speak, apparently interchangeably, of the Spirit within and being in the Spirit, so too he speaks not only of Christ within but also of being *in Christ.* Indeed, the last is by far the most common expression he uses.[33] For that very reason, though, the phrase is more difficult to assess. It occurs so frequently in Paul's letters that a reasonably complete survey is not possible; the meaning Paul attaches to it seems to vary; and its point of contact—if any—with similar Greco-Roman concepts is debated and dubious. Yet it is widely regarded as the central element of Paul's mysticism.[34]

The frequency of the phrase dulls its impact. The modern reader tends to skip over it as pious filler. Certainly Paul often uses the phrase in ways that do not emphasize or even necessarily suggest Christ as a *place* where one exists. Thus, for example, in the space of thirteen verses in his letter to the Philippians he claims to hope *in the Lord Jesus* to send Timothy to them (2:19) and to trust *in the Lord* that he would also come (2:24), and he urges them to welcome Epaphroditus *in the Lord* (2:29) and to rejoice *in the Lord* (3:1). He also addresses the letter to the saints *in Christ Jesus* (1:1) and closes by greeting every saint *in Christ Jesus* (5:21). Additionally he uses the phrase frequently to reinforce the authority of his own words: "We ask and urge you *in the Lord Jesus*" (1 Thess 4:1; see also Rom 9:1; 2 Cor 12:19). But within this varied and ubiquitous usage are statements that seem to point to the experienced reality that underlies Paul's fondness for the phrase.

> More than that, I regard everything as loss because of the surpassing value of knowing Christ Jesus my Lord. For his sake I have suffered the loss of all things, and I regard them as rubbish, in order that I may gain Christ and be found *in him*. (Phil 3:8–9a)

> So if anyone is *in Christ*, there is a new creation: everything old has passed away; see, everything has become new! (2 Cor 5:17)

> I know a person *in Christ* who fourteen years ago was caught up to the third heaven—whether in the body or out of the body I do not know; God knows. (2 Cor 12:2)

> As many of you as were baptized into Christ have clothed yourselves with Christ. There is no longer Jew or Greek, there is no longer slave or free, there is no longer male and female; for all of you are one *in Christ Jesus*. (Gal 3:27–28)

Some, of course, deny any mystical meaning even to these statements. Bultmann insisted that Paul's references to being "in Christ" meant no more than later references to being a Christian, a member of the ecclesial body of Christ. But is that all it means? Dunn says no: "Paul evidently felt himself to be caught up 'in Christ' and borne along by Christ."[35] Pelser agrees: "[Paul] must certainly be talking about a reality that lies beyond the reality of this world ruled by natural senses."[36]

Much effort has been expended on attempts to identify the background of the concept of participating in Christ or in the body of Christ. What in the Greco-Roman world resembled these claims? What known concepts could Paul's hearers and readers have drawn upon to grasp the significance of his words? What known concepts might have influenced Paul to express himself this way? Three suggestions are regularly offered: the gnostic redeemer myth, the Jewish concept of corporate personality, and the initiation rites of the mystery cults.[37]

The gnostic myth concerns the fate of a "heavenly man" out of whose substance individual humans were created and with whom these individuals (more precisely, the heavenly portions of these individuals) are ultimately reunited.[38] This myth, however, is known only from sources much later than Paul and thus is an unlikely source for Paul's language or his hearers' understanding. "Corporate personality" embraces the Old Testament idea that "one can represent many"[39] so that the deed of one becomes the deed of those he represents (see esp. Gen 12:3; Rom 4:11–12; 5:12–21). However, the concept that dominates the notion of corporate personality in that of representation, which seems a far cry from the notions of union and incorporation that Paul's language suggests.[40] The mystery rites may have involved a ritual union with the deity, but details are elusive (see below). Overall, though, this line of analysis seems to have reached a dead end, with no consensus having emerged. Failure to identify the background of Paul's language of participation does not, however, mean that Paul could not be referring to real participation. It simply reinforces the need to be attentive to Paul's own words.

Baptized into Christ, baptized into his death, crucified with Christ. Twice Paul refers to being "baptized into Christ" (Rom 6:3; Gal 3:27). The phrase can be interpreted in a variety of ways. In one line of interpretation the phrase is regarded as an abbreviated form of "baptized into [or: in] the name of Christ."[41] Paul does not use that longer form, but he seems to presuppose knowledge of it when he asks (sarcastically), "Were you baptized into [Greek *eis*] the name of Paul?" (1 Cor 1:13; see also 1:15). If this is the background and meaning of the phrase "baptized into Christ," then that phrase has no mystical or participatory overtones. It proclaims, as the more fulsome formula does, that the baptized person now belongs to Christ.[42]

The phrase can also be interpreted as a reference to the baptized person's incorporation into the body of Christ, but this metaphor is a fluid and slippery one. Sometimes the body of Christ seems to refer to the church as a collective entity identified by its allegiance to Christ (e.g., 1 Cor 12:27).

Baptism into *this* body refers to the rite of initiation into this community of faith. Other times, however, the body of Christ seems to suggest a "mystical" entity (1 Cor 10:16).[43] In Gal 3:27 Paul equates being baptized into Christ with "putting on Christ," a striking phrase that suggests an intimate union with Christ.[44] On this reading being baptized into Christ refers to the act of mystical union with him.[45]

Paul's reference to being baptized into Christ's death (Rom 6:3) and the similar comment about being crucified with Christ (Gal 2:19) are even more difficult and disputed.[46] The prevailing tendency has been to treat these words as similes, so that they are understood to mean dying *as* Christ died (in baptism?) and suffering *as* Christ suffered on the cross (through rejection or social ostracism?).[47] Certainly Paul's words in Rom 6:5 ("for if we have been united with him in a death *like* his . . .") and his catalogs of apostolic sufferings (Phil 1:12–26; 2 Cor 11:22–30) would seem to support this conclusion. Yet several passages also support a participatory or mystical interpretation: dying (and rising) by becoming one with Christ.[48] In 2 Cor 5:14, for example, Paul follows his assertion that "we are convinced that one has died for all," not with a reference to the atoning power of that death, but with a conclusion that makes most sense if one assumes a mystical or participatory element in Paul's logic: "therefore all have died."[49] Similarly, the assertion "I have been crucified with Christ" (Gal 2:19) is followed immediately by a second assertion that strongly suggests union with Christ: "And it is no longer I who live, but it is Christ who lives in me." The upshot of all this is that scholars who accept on other grounds a mystical component to Paul's thought are inclined (but not obligated) to find allusions to mystical participation in these passages about baptism into Christ and into his death. Those not inclined toward a mystical interpretation of Paul can find grounds for denying it here.

Much attention has been given to the possible origin of the language of baptism into Christ's death or, more generally, the concept of dying and rising with Christ. The Hellenistic mystery cults, with their myths of dying and rising or rejuvenated gods,[50] have long been regarded as the conceptual background, if not the actual origin, of Paul's language. Flaws have been found with this theory, though, sufficient to cause most scholars to abandon it.[51] There is apparently no reference to being baptized into Isis, for example, nor any indication that the initiate died, was buried, or raised "with" Osiris.[52] There is even some debate over whether the initiate was even identified with the cult god or goddess. Dunn, for example, unequivocally says no; Pelser, though, claims that "devotees are in some way identified with the cult deity," though he refuses to call it a "mystical union."[53] The problem is that texts from or about these cults are few and notoriously ambiguous and difficult to interpret. (The "mystery cults" got their name, after all, from the fact that the rites were a carefully guarded secret.) It is important, however, to distinguish between what actually happened in the cultic rites and the popular perception of the cult practices. Brook Pearson argues that there is "more than enough evidence to suggest that the connection between baptism, death (symbolic, actual, or simply the possibility thereof) and initiation into the cult of Isis would have existed in at least the popular mind."[54] That would be sufficient.

The debate is obviously not over, though Dunn's suggestion that the metaphor of baptism into Jesus' death originated in Jesus' own reference to his death as a "baptism I am to be baptized with" (Mark 10:38) has much to commend it.[55] However, knowledge of the origin of Paul's language of baptism into Christ and into his death is not essential for assessing the presence or absence of a mystical element in Paul's thought, for on any hypothesis it is a concept that Paul himself further developed.

What Does It Mean?

The most frequently encountered explanation is that the language of participation is to be understood metaphorically (e.g., the body of Christ is a metaphor for the church)[56] or as a simile (e.g., we experience something like Christ's death). But what would it mean to assume that the language of participation in Christ refers to just that: participation in Christ? It is important first to address some common misconceptions. Paul's mysticism was Christ-mysticism; he did not focus, as later mystics did, on mystical union with God (but see Phil 2:13). Moreover, mysticism, if it is present, does not in Paul's letters imply a union with Christ that somehow makes the person divine, nor does it mean that the person is dissolved into Christ so completely that his or her personhood is obliterated. It was the assumption that "mysticism" necessarily implied these things that led to a reluctance to use this term to describe what Paul was talking about. But if being "in Christ" or having Christ "in you" did not imply absorption into Christ, it did imply, as Pelser insists, "more than entering into a special relationship with Christ." His attempt to describe the phenomenon is as good as any: "It is rather the coming about of a totally new form of existence, an existence of being fully controlled by Christ, of living through Christ living in the believer. It is the coming about of a new personality in which Christ can be identified, yet without the believer losing her/his identity. It is a union between Christ and the believer, established by Christ and experienced through faith in him, that can probably be best described as 'mystical.'"[57] In addition, though, it was not, at least as Paul developed it, a purely individualistic phenomenon, and it had a distinctively eschatological component: union with Christ experienced in this world was only a fore-taste of the Parousia.

Paul referred to this mystical union at key points in his letters, often when he was speaking of ethics: participation in Christ necessitated or enabled certain modes of behavior (Rom 6:3–4). Those who have "put on" Christ have put on his way of life as well (Gal 5:22–26). He also drew on this concept to emphasize the inclusive quality of their new existence: Jews and Gentiles together are in Christ Jesus (Gal 3:26–27), and "we *who are many* are one body" (1 Cor 10:17). And he often described salvation in terms of participation in Christ. Those in union with Christ share in his righteousness (1 Cor 1:30), participate in his death (Rom 6:13), and are raised in him to a new life (1 Cor 5:17).[58] To be sure, Paul does not present this as an inalterable reality. His many warnings and exhortations indicate clearly enough that however real he understood the union with Christ to be, he did not understand it as a union that could not be broken by failure to live out that union, to document it through one's actions. As he says, Christ must be "formed" in them (Gal 4:19).

It is important to note that this is not the only way that Paul thought of Christ. Paul was, as Schweitzer noted, "not wholly and solely a mystic,"[59] that is, he did not always use the language and logic of mysticism in his letters. He also spoke, especially when he was addressing the problem of the Jewish law, in legal terms of Christ's death as an atonement sacrifice that permitted the righteous God to pass over (overlook) humanity's sins (Rom 3:24–26; see also 4:25; Gal 3:13).[60] It has long been conceded that these two modes of thought, juridical (legal) and mystical, coexisted rather uneasily and illogically in Paul's letters. Faith in Christ is central to one, union with Christ to the other. The tension is significantly reduced, however, if, as many now argue, Paul's understanding of faith also had a participatory element. That topic requires its own chapter (see chapter 3).

An additional implication of taking seriously Paul's language of participation concerns the sense of self rather than the sense of salvation. It seems an obvious conclusion that union with or participation in Christ should change one's sense of identity. Dale Martin's interpretation of Paul's rebuke of certain men who were visiting prostitutes (1 Cor 6:15–20) highlights that consequence:

The Christian man's being is defined by his participation in the body of Christ. "Do you not know that your bodies are members of Christ? Will I therefore take the members of Christ and make them members of a prostitute? Absolutely not!" (6:15). The pneumatic union between the body of the Christian man and the body of Christ (6:17) is what identifies the Christian man. The man's body and Christ's body share the same pneuma; the man's body is therefore an appendage of Christ's body, totally dependent on the pneumatic life-force of the larger body for its existence.[61]

Was the body of Christ in which the men participated perceived to be gendered? A startling question, perhaps, but some answer that it was, and argue as well that when Paul asserted that in Christ Jesus there is no longer male and female (Gal 3:28), he was not proclaiming the equality of men and women in Christ. Rather, "believers are no longer male and female inasmuch as they have become one *male* person."[62] If this is true, it raises an interesting question: What would it have meant to the women of Paul's churches to be told that their bodies were members of Christ? More precisely, What would it have meant to them to be told that their female bodies were members of the male Christ?[63]

Paul does not address this question, but his letters may provide an indirect answer. In the Greco-Roman world sexuality was understood not as a dichotomy between male and female but as a continuum of possibilities. This was not a horizontal continuum. There was a top and a bottom to it, with the male end of the spectrum (associated with strength, rationality, self-control, activity, and perfection) exercising a natural dominance over the female end (associated with weakness, sexuality and procreation, passion, passivity, and imperfection). Each human body comprised male and female aspects, and depending on the relative strength of these aspects each individual could be located at a different point along the male-female axis. Moreover, under the influence of certain internal or external forces, male or female aspects could be enhanced. When this occurred, an individual could move along the spectrum, either slipping downward to greater femininity or rising to a greater degree of masculinity.

Thus passages once read as evidence of the egalitarian ethos of the early church can just as easily be read as evidence that the self-definition of women who experienced the indwelling presence of Christ was shifted toward the male end of the spectrum. With Christ in them (or they in Christ) women may have felt more empowered as male. In particular, the preference for celibacy and virginity that is well attested in

Corinth (1 Cor 7) and present still in second-century Pauline churches (1 Tim 5:3–16) was, for the women involved, a rejection of culturally prescribed female roles in favor of a more ambiguous status. The actions of the women who discarded their veils (1 Cor 11:2–16) may have been motivated at some level by a new sense of (masculine) invulnerability to the hostile spiritual forces against which the veils had protected them. Certainly the actions were a rejection of cultural norms of distinctively female dress and decorum. Paul's rebuke of women in 1 Cor 14:34–35 (if it is authentic) shows them to have been engaged in the active, public roles typically reserved for men. Actions not linked explicitly to women, but not linked exclusively to men either, contribute to this evidence of a "masculinization" of the congregation: the Corinthian claim to authority (4:6); to wisdom, strength, and honor (4:10); to freedom (9:1); and to knowledge (8:1).

There is evidence from the second century that becoming male was for women a plausible, desired, and occasionally necessary part of Christian self-definition.[64] It is, of course, highly speculative to suggest it, but the actions of women that Paul discusses in his letter to the Corinthians may provide evidence that in that first-century culture as well the experience of union with Christ altered their sense of self in a masculine direction. Certainly their actions *in Christ* would have been regarded as more appropriate to men than to women.

Conclusion

Was Paul a mystic, and did union with Christ play an important role in his thought and letters? The excesses of the claims of the early proponents of this idea are often noted and probably contributed to its widespread rejection, but those who rejected it were also excessive in their zeal to purge any hint of mysticism from Paul's words. Paul describes his conversion in mystical terms ("God . . . was pleased to reveal his Son *in* me")[65] and reports as a third-person account a clearly mystical experience that was probably his own (2 Cor 12:1–5). Throughout his letters is language that, if taken at face value, seems to refer to a union with Christ that is best described as mystical. Moreover, as Dunn notes, "study of participation in Christ leads more directly into the rest of Paul's theology than justification"[66]—that is, it seems to be more foundational to his thought.

Paul does not argue the case that union with Christ is a central part of the believer's experience. He *assumes* it, and assumes as well that his readers have experienced this union and will understand his arguments that are based on allusions to that experience. This concept of salvation through mystical union with Christ may, however, make Paul's message less accessible to modern readers who have had no similar experience. It may seem to them foreign, strange, and irrelevant. Others, however, may rejoice to find in Paul a line of thought that does not center on the notion that God requires a sacrifice in order to redeem humanity. The starting point, though, should be Paul's words, not modern preferences; and many of those words seem to be the words of a true mystic. He did not, however, retreat into that mystical union in isolation from the world, but found there the strength to engage daily in his very nonmystical struggle to establish, nurture, correct, and comfort cells of believers in the Roman world.

Chapter Five

The Righteousness of God

If Paul had not written Romans, one would never suspect that God's righteousness was of any particular theological importance to him. He mentions it once in a curious statement in 2 Corinthians ("For our sake he made him to be sin who knew no sin, so that in him we might become the righteousness of God," 5:21),[1] but nowhere else in his letters—apart from Romans—does the phrase "the righteousness of God" appear. The word "righteousness" is, of course, abundantly present,[2] and there is one verse in which righteousness is described as *"from* God" (Phil 3:9; implicit also in 1 Cor 1:30), but apart from 2 Cor 5:21 there are no references to the righteousness *of* God—until you turn to Romans.

In Romans Paul refers to God's righteousness eight times.[3] He introduces the concept in the opening words of the body of the letter (1:16–17), linking it directly to the gospel. He mentions it again in 3:5, dwells on it at some length (4 times) in a pivotal passage (3:21–26), and evokes it again (2 times) as he explores the dilemma of Israel in the closing chapters of his theological exposition (10:3). God's righteousness, virtually ignored in all previous letters, is the *theme* of this final letter,[4] and that raises a couple of interesting questions. What does Paul mean by this phrase? And if God's righteousness is so central to the gospel, why did he mention it only in Romans?

Debates over the meaning of the phrase (and they have been legion) are rooted in the ambiguity of the Greek. The phrase in question consists of one noun, *dikaiosynē* (usually translated "righteousness"), modified—that is, more closely defined—by a second noun, *theos* (God), in the genitive case (*theou*). The problem is that the genitive case in Greek is very flexible: it can relate the second noun to the first in a number of ways.

49

The most common use of the genitive is to indicate possession of a thing or quality, or, if the first noun designates an action, to indicate the doer of that action. (The second nuance is designated a subjective genitive.) This is reflected in the translation "the righteousness of God" or "God's righteousness," though it leaves unresolved the question of whether *dikaiosynē* represents an attribute or an action of God. The genitive can also indicate the *object* of the action designated by the first noun, which would result in a meaning roughly equivalent to "the righteousness that is valid before God."[5] As a third option, the genitive can indicate origin or authorship, so that *dikaiosynē theou* would designate "the righteousness that goes forth from God" or, more specifically, "God's gift of righteousness." The range of nuances possible for the noun *dikaiosynē* adds to the difficulty of establishing what Paul meant by the phrase,[6] and there is the further question of whether, given all this flexibility, he always meant the same thing.

Background

A defining moment in the discussion of the meaning of the phrase was an interchange between Rudolf Bultmann and his former student Ernst Käsemann on this topic. Bultmann equated "God's righteousness" with the righteousness that God reckons to those who have faith; that is, he took it as a genitive of authorship. The phrase "God's righteousness" is thus, in his view, another way of talking about justification. "It is God-given, God-adjudicated righteousness," pure and simple.[7] Käsemann countered with the claim that although the "general tenor" of Paul's comments on *dikaiosynē theou* favors its interpretation as gift,[8] that cannot be all that Paul meant. If it were, he said, there would be no reason for Paul to refer to "God's righteousness" (that is, to use the genitive construction) and not to speak more clearly and consistently of the righteousness *from* God (using a prepositional phrase, as in Phil 3:9). Thus, says Käsemann, Paul intended the phrase *dikaiosynē theou* to convey not simply the gift of righteousness, but also to characterize God's own activity and nature. "God's righteousness," he says, is primarily a reference to God's saving activity, to God's power that brings salvation to pass, a power that is also present in the gift. It is not simply gift, but power *and* gift, and the genitive is thus understood as both subjective genitive (power) and genitive of origin (gift).[9]

This exchange of opinions[10] was important not because it provided the final word on the topic. Rather, the energy of the debate, and in particular Käsemann's introduction of a fresh perspective (God's power) into the debate, sparked renewed interest in the topic and further research.[11] Of the many salient results of that research, expanded knowledge of the Jewish background of the concept and greater methodological sophistication in dealing with Paul's letters and theology are among the most important.

Jewish background. References to God's *ṣedeq* or *ṣĕdāqâ*, the nearest Hebrew equivalents to the Greek *dikaiosynē*, are particularly prominent in the Psalms and Isaiah 40–66.[12] The root meaning of *ṣedeq* and *ṣĕdāqâ* (the two terms are essentially synonymous) conveys rightness and justice, but the words appear in connection with other terms that clarify and focus their meaning.

In Psalm 99 *ṣĕdāqâ*, "righteousness," is associated with God's role as cosmic ruler and judge:

> Mighty King, lover of justice (*mišpāṭ*),
>   you have established equity (*mēšārîm*);
> you have executed justice
>   and righteousness (*ṣĕdāqâ*) in Jacob.
> Extol the LORD our God;
>   worship at his footstool.
>   Holy is he!
>   (Ps 99:4–5; see also 96:13; 97:2; 98:9)

In psalms such as this one, *ṣĕdāqâ* is linked with, and assumes the nuance of, legal justice (*mišpāṭ*) and the associated juridical qualities of equity or fairness (9:8; 98:9; 99:4), truth (*ʾĕmûnâ*, Ps 96:13), and also forgiveness (99:8). Other texts add that God's justice involves impartiality and integrity (Deut 10:17; Ps 82:1–4; 2 Chr 19:7; Job 34:17–19).

God's attribute of justice was known, of course, through events that were understood to be God's active and just intervention on behalf of the nation of Israel or of individuals (especially poor or vulnerable individuals) within that nation. In other texts God's intervention on Israel's behalf, still celebrated or invoked as evidence of divine righteousness, was linked more with God's covenant relationship with Israel than with God's role as cosmic judge.

> I have told the glad news of *ṣedeq*
>   in the great congregation;
> see, I have not restrained my lips,
>   as you know, O LORD.

I have not hidden your *ṣĕdāqâ* within my heart,
   I have spoken of your faithfulness (*ʾĕmûnâ*) and your salvation (*tĕšûʿâ*)
I have not concealed your steadfast love (*ḥesed*) and your faithfulness
  (*ʾĕmet*)[13]
   from the great congregation.
Do not, O LORD, withhold
   your mercy (*raḥămîm*) from me;
let your steadfast love (*ḥesed*) and your faithfulness (*ʾĕmet*)
   keep me safe forever.
              (Ps 40:9–11; vv. 10–12 Heb. See also 33:4–5; 36:5–6)

Legal language is absent here; instead, God's *ṣedeq/ṣĕdāqâ* is mentioned in parallelism with faithfulness, steadfast love, and loyalty, all covenant terms. In the context of this psalm, which includes a cry for deliverance, the dominant nuance of *ṣedeq/ṣĕdāqâ* is the rightness of God's saving action in faithfulness to the covenant people.

The contexts of the various psalms are not always clear, but that of Isa 40–55 (Deutero-Isaiah) is. Written in Babylon toward the end of the exile, this work extols God's *ṣedeq/ṣĕdāqâ* in a slightly different key. In Isa 51, for example, God's *ṣedeq* is repeatedly paired with references to God's impending saving action (*yĕšûʿâ*, vv. 5, 6, 8) on behalf of "my people" or "my nation" (v. 4). The relationship between God and the people is developed at great length: their origin is in God (the rock from which they were hewn, v. 1); they have received God's Torah, which dwells in their hearts (v. 7); they are heirs of the blessing and promise that God gave to Abraham (v. 2). They have already experienced God's aid "in days of old," especially at the parting of the waters of the Red Sea (vv. 9–10). Through the voice of the prophet, God proclaims that Israel's sure hope for future deliverance lies in this enduring relationship, which includes promise, exodus, and covenant. Because of God's *ṣedeq*, God has acted faithfully, steadfastly, and repeatedly on behalf of God's people. The prophet is confident that now, when God's people are exiled in Babylon, God's *ṣedeq* will result in another saving action for Israel. Yet there is more. The prophet envisions the cosmic dimensions of this *ṣedeq*, which will embrace not only "my people," the covenant people, but will overflow in eschatological triumph for "the peoples"—that is, the Gentiles—as well (vv. 4–5).

What, then, does *ṣedeq/ṣĕdāqâ* mean in Deutero-Isaiah? Scullion asserts that "Yahweh's *ṣĕdāqâ* is his saving action,"[14] and the words *ṣedeq* and *ṣĕdāqâ* are translated "deliverance" in the NRSV (vv. 5, 6, 8).[15] Such definitions and translations are, however, problematic for two reasons. First, they obscure the fact that the root meaning of *ṣedeq* and *ṣĕdāqâ* has to do with the notion of "rightness" or "righteousness" and replace this concept with words that refer to the outcome of that righteousness. There is, as Williams asserts, a necessary distinction to be made between the divine attribute of righteousness and the manifestations of that attribute through acts of deliverance:

> These words ["steadfast love," "faithfulness," "goodness"] are intended to designate the nature of God, and they are all covenant terms, that is, they describe God as he is known in covenant relationship with Israel. Of course Yahweh's *ḥesed*, *ʾĕmûnâh*, *ʾĕmet* and *ṭûb* are known only as God *acts* on behalf of his people, but this does not mean that these words *designate* deeds or activity. They characterize the being of the God who makes himself known in deeds; they point to aspects of the divine nature. So, too, does the word "righteousness."[16]

Second, they equate *ṣedeq* or *ṣĕdāqâ* with one of the other terms (in this instance *yĕšûʿâ*) closely associated with it in the passage, thus ignoring Scullion's own dictum: "*Ṣedeq* and *ṣĕdāqâ* are not identical with these words; rather the parallels complement and intensify each other or their meanings overlap or both."[17] Even if the meanings "overlap," the contextual definition or translation of *ṣedeq/ṣĕdāqâ* should convey the particular semantic contribution of these words.[18] That is, in a passage filled with overlapping terms, each has a role to play in conveying the nature of "a multi-faceted action" of God. *Ṣedeq* and *ṣĕdāqâ* contribute the notion of the rightness of this action, and that contribution should be acknowledged in any definition or translation.

For Deutero-Isaiah, then, *ṣedeq* and *ṣĕdāqâ* are not identical to deliverance, but their presence in a word field filled with references to salvation and covenant faithfulness intensifies the notion that God's righteousness is rightly and reliably and faithfully manifested in saving acts on behalf of God's covenant people. But because Deutero-Isaiah celebrates the cosmic dimensions of God's dominion (see, e.g., Isa 40:12–17), God's righteousness will extend these saving acts to embrace the Gentiles as well.

The scrolls found in the caves of Khirbet Qumran near the Dead Sea contain many references to God's *ṣedeq/ṣĕdāqâ*. These scrolls were written or preserved by a sectarian Jewish community with strongly dualistic views and an equally strong sense of individual election and predestination. Those who were members of this sect were not born into it; each joined by a conscious decision, which was, however, understood to reflect their prior election by God. By joining with this community and so fulfilling their predestined lot, they escaped the fate of the wicked (which included all Jews who were not members of this sect) and became one of the elect, the children of righteousness. Within this group of sectarians, God's righteousness acquired nuances that sound remarkably Pauline.[19]

> As for me,
>   my justification is with God.
> In His hand are the perfection of my way
>   and the uprightness of my heart.
> He will wipe out my transgression through His righteousness.
>
> ——
>
> From the source of His righteousness
>   is my justification,
> and from His marvellous mysteries
>   is the light in my heart.
> My eyes have gazed on that which is eternal,
> on wisdom concealed from men,
>   on knowledge and wise design
>   (hidden) from the sons of men;
> on a fountain of righteousness
>   and on a storehouse of power.
>
> ——
>
> For mankind has no way,
>   and man is unable to establish his steps
> since justification is with God
>   and perfection of way is out of His hand.
> All things come to pass by His knowledge;
> He establishes all things by His design
>   and without Him nothing is done.
> As for me,
>   if I stumble, the mercies of God
>   shall be my eternal salvation.
> If I stagger because of the sin of flesh,
>   my justification shall be
>   by the righteousness of God which endures for ever.
>
> ——
>
> He will judge me in the righteousness of His truth
>   and in the greatness of His goodness

He will pardon all my sins.
Through His righteousness He will cleanse me
   of the uncleanness of man
   and of the sins of the children of men,
that I may confess to God His righteousness,
   and His majesty to the Most High.
(1QS 11:2–15)

When the elect are in view in these documents, the words that surround and interpret the references to God's righteousness emphasize power, but also grace, mercy, compassion, forgiveness, goodness, and especially the mystery of election. God's righteousness lies at the heart of this mystery, which has been revealed to these favored individuals:

Blessed art Thou, O Lord,
   Maker [of all things and mighty in] deeds:
   all things are Thy work!
Behold, Thou art pleased to favour [Thy servant],
   and hast graced me with Thy spirit of mercy
   and [with the radiance] of Thy glory.
Thine, Thine is righteousness,
   for it is Thou who hast done all [these things]!
(1QH 16:8–9)[20]

This examination of some scriptural passages and Qumran texts that refer to God's righteousness has been undertaken for several reasons. First, when Paul introduces the concept in his letter to the Romans, he does not explain it, and so he must have assumed that the recipients, whom he had never met, already had some knowledge of it, most probably from scripture.[21] In addition, though, these texts show that the concept was not static. It had some basic connotations—divine "rightness" revealed in acts of justice and deliverance—but it acquired different nuances or dimensions in different contexts.[22] Finally, the texts demonstrate that the way the concept was nuanced was by surrounding it with related terms and concepts that expanded or focused or otherwise shaped its meaning for that context. Paul, it turns out, did the same thing.

Methodological considerations. Given the fact that all (save one) of the references to *dikaiosynē theou* occur in Romans, it seems obvious that one should focus on that letter to determine what Paul meant by the phrase. Yet Bultmann's textual starting point for arguing that *dikaiosynē theou* refers to God's *gift* of righteousness was Phil 3:9, a verse that contains the similar but nevertheless significantly different phrase, "the righteousness that is from God" (*tēn ek theou dikaiosynēn*).[23] Käsemann also accepted Phil 3:9 as the key for interpreting *dikaiosynē theou* as a genitive of origin, but his primary contribution to the debate was to define God's righteousness as God's power. His textual starting point was Rom 1:17, which certainly associates the revelation of God's righteousness in the gospel with the power of God contained in that gospel. Käsemann, however, has turned this association into a virtual equation.[24] The real problem, however, is more fundamental.

Both Bultmann and Käsemann, as well as the many scholars who have embraced variants of their views, have worked with the tacit assumption that almost the whole of Paul's theology of justification is compressed into the phrase *dikaiosynē theou*.[25] This seems a dubious assumption. Certainly, according to Paul, righteousness, a right relationship with God, is a gift from God, and Paul has several clear ways of expressing that. He uses the verb *dikaioun* ("to justify") to refer to God's activity of setting persons into right relationship with Godself (e.g., Rom 3:24; Gal 2:16), and he uses prepositional phrases (Greek *ek* or *apo*) to refer unambiguously to the righteousness that derives from God (e.g., Phil 3:9; 1 Cor 1:30).[26] Paul also discusses the righteous behavior that is acceptable to God, again in clear language (e.g., Rom 3:10–18; 6:12–13, 16–20).[27] Paul certainly holds these concepts together as part of a larger conceptual whole, but it does not follow that he uses the single phrase *dikaiosynē theou* to embrace them all. Within this conceptual whole, the phrase *dikaiosynē theou* seems to refer to an important aspect of God's nature, an aspect that Williams describes as "God's steadfast adherence to what is right and fitting, his constancy, his trustworthiness and his readiness to save."[28] Yet even this description gets a bit ahead of the game. In Romans Paul draws on *various* understandings and applications of the concept of God's righteousness—including some that focus on God's rigorous and punitive justice—in order to move toward the understanding of the concept that undergirds his message in this letter. It is not so much by determining *what* "God's righteousness" means as by investigating *how* it means in Romans that we can gain real insight into its significance for Paul. To keep our focus on this *process*, the starting definition must be more basic: God's readiness to do what is right and fitting.[29] It remains to be seen how Paul enlarges this basic meaning in light of the gospel, and especially in light of the very particular shape of his message to the churches in Rome.

The Righteousness of God in Romans

Romans 1:16–3:20. After the opening salutation and prayer, standard features of Paul's letters, Paul makes the transition into the body of the letter with the following words:

> For I am not ashamed of the gospel; it is the power of God for salvation to everyone who believes [or: trusts], to the Jew first and also to the Greek. For in it the righteousness of God is being revealed from faith for faith; as it is written, "The one who is righteous will live from faith." (Rom 1:16–17 NRSV, alt.)[30]

Here, in a passage that provides the initial statement of the theme of the letter, Paul introduces the concept of the righteousness of God. He does not define it, but readers familiar with Jewish scripture would recognize certain associations. As occasionally in the Psalms and Deutero-Isaiah, God's righteousness is associated with an active manifestation of God's power.[31] Moreover, this power is for *salvation*, another component of the word field that frequently surrounds and helps focus references to God's righteousness in Jewish writings. There are also several references to faith or faithfulness (the Greek word *pistis* has both meanings), and though Paul does not specifically identify any as God's faithfulness, it is very likely that "from faith" means "from [God's] faithfulness."[32] Since this constellation of clarifying terms generally evokes the notion of God's righteousness worked out in demonstrations of covenant loyalty to Israel, it would have been somewhat surprising to an audience familiar with that notion that Paul identifies the objects of God's saving power, and thus the beneficiaries of God's righteousness, as "everyone who trusts [or: believes], the Jew of course, but *also* the Greek."[33] There were hints of this universal reach of God's righteousness as an eschatological hope in Jewish writings, but its prominence here is striking. In the thematic introduction to the letter, Paul asserts that God's righteousness is *now* active to include the Gentiles.[34]

The issues introduced with such brevity here are more fully developed in 3:21–31, but in the intervening verses Paul continues to explore and expand the significance of the righteousness of God. He does so, though, by discussing concepts that highlight the juridical or legal implications of the phrase. First he associates the righteousness of God with the wrath of God by using the same verb ("is being revealed") with both. Here wrath designates not an emotion but the way God's steadfast adherence to what is right and fitting is revealed in the context of, and in response to, willful ungodliness and wickedness (lit. "unrighteousness"). This passage (1:18–32) not only emphasizes that God's righteousness includes just punishment (the justness being emphasized by the way the punishment is made to fit the crime);[35] it also declares again the universal reach of God's righteousness: against *all* ungodliness. The opening salvo is against *Gentile* ungodliness, but implicitly in 2:1 and explicitly in 2:9 Jews are included.[36]

Chapter 2 intensifies the focus on the way God's *dikaiosynē* manifests itself as justice, echoing themes familiar from the Psalms. God's justice is in accordance with truth (v. 2; cf. Ps 96:13). God's justice is righteous (v. 5; cf. Ps 98:9). God's justice includes kindness, forbearance, and patience—but only up to a certain point (v. 4; see esp. 1QS11). God's justice is fair (vv. 6–10; cf. Ps 99:4); God's justice is impartial (v. 11; cf. Ps 82:1–4). And—emphatically—God's justice embraces impartially both Jew and Greek (vv. 9–10).

This last point is obviously important to Paul, for he develops it at some length (vv. 12–29). Possession of the law, God's law, by one group and not the other does not compromise the equity of God's justice, for "it is not the hearers of the law who are righteous in God's sight, but the doers of the law" (v. 13), and Gentiles can "do instinctively what the law requires" (v. 14). Nor does the special relationship that Jews have with God, signaled by the rite of circumcision, create favoritism in God's justice. Circumcision is of value only if one obeys the law, and "if those who are uncircumcised keep the requirements of the law, will not their uncircumcision be regarded as circumcision?" (v. 25).

Paul has developed the aspect of God's strict and impartial justice to the point that God's covenant loyalty, another way in which God's righteousness finds expression, seems to have been left far behind. Paul articulates the obvious question that his argument has raised: "What advantage has the Jew?" His answer is both surprising and obscure. It is surprising because, after arguing at great length that the Jewish law, Jewish circumcision, and by implication the Jewish covenant do not provide any advantage in God's just judgment, Paul now states that the Jewish advantage is "much in every way." It is obscure because Paul seems to have an extensive list in mind ("in the first place"), but he cites only a single point (3:2). Moreover, he follows this with a series of questions that move farther and farther from the stated goal of demonstrating that the Jews have a real advantage.[37] What the questions do accomplish, though, is to bring *dikaiosynē theou* (translated here in the NRSV as "the justice of

God") explicitly back into the argument and to reinforce the connection between this concept and the covenantal concepts of God's faithfulness and God's truth.

Paul presents three contrasting pairs:

their (some Jews') faithlessness (*apistia*)	God's faithfulness (*pistis*)
our (probably the Gentiles') injustice (*adikia*)	God's *dikaiosynē*
my (Paul's?) falsehood (*pseusma*)	God's truth (*alētheia*)

The shifting pronouns—"their, our, my"—on the human side are interesting and not entirely clear,[38] but it is clear that the three attributes ascribed to God are related. "Faithfulness" and "truth" (which probably conveys fidelity or constancy, as in Ps 40 above) evoke once again the idea that God's *dikaiosynē* manifests itself as covenant loyalty, though the word "covenant" is strangely absent.[39] Moreover, notions of covenant loyalty are overlaid with notions of legal justice (see, e.g., vv. 5–6), so that covenant loyalty and righteous judgment are simultaneously evoked.

The word that Paul uses to describe the object of the Jew's faithlessness and God's faithfulness is *logia*, variously translated as "oracles" (NRSV), "utterances" (NAB), or "message" (NJB). Paul describes the relationship of the Jews to the *logia* not in terms of their being bound or obligated (as to a covenant, see Gal 4:21—5:5) but in terms of their being entrusted with them. That is, the *logia* were to be held in trust—by implication, for others. At this point in the argument Paul does not indicate the intended beneficiaries of this trust; he notes instead that some of the Jews have failed in their fiduciary responsibility. Thus, though the concepts of faithfulness, righteousness, and truthfulness are linked to covenant ideology, and through that to the notion of God's saving intervention on behalf of the covenant people, Paul's argument pushes them subtly in a different direction.

Sam Williams argues that the *logia* are the promises of God to Abraham and not, as most assume, God's covenant promises to Israel. These promises are summarized in Gen 12:3, quoted in Gal 3:8: "In you shall all the nations [i.e., Gentiles] be blessed." Williams thus concludes that in Rom 3:1–7 Paul "virtually 'defines' *dikaiosynē theou* for his readers . . . [as] God's faithfulness to his promises to Abraham, promises which focus upon the eschatological gathering of all the nations into the people of God."[40] Readers who had skipped ahead to chapter 4 of the letter, or readers acquainted with Galatians, might grasp this definition in Rom 3. But for most, Paul's argument would unfold more slowly and less directly.

In the next section of the letter (3:9–20) Paul cites a string of scripture quotations to establish the point that in the present circumstances, "No one is righteous, no not one" (v. 10), that is, no one stands in the relationship with God that will result in salvation. This in turn sets the stage for Paul to return to and explicate his opening claim that the gospel is the power of God for salvation to everyone who has faith, and that this gospel of salvation reveals the righteousness of God (3:21–31) in a new light. Before we explore this passage, it will be helpful to summarize once again the intervening argument as it touches on the concept of God's *dikaiosynē*.

After the initial thematic statement (1:16–17), which introduces the divine attribute of *dikaiosynē*, Paul describes in familiar ways how that attribute is revealed in God's acts of righteous judgment. However, he pushes the notion of the impartiality of God's righteous justice to such radical limits that it challenges, indeed undermines, the traditional view that God's *dikaiosynē* is also manifested in God's steadfast loyalty to the covenant with Israel. The series of questions in 3:1–7 demonstrates how far Paul seems to have destabilized the familiar concept. The defense of God's righteousness that he offers there is emphatic but inadequate. Much of the rest of the letter is devoted to showing how God's righteousness is now revealed in the gospel, that is, what aspects are manifested by God's actions in this new context and how this new revelation comports with traditional views.

Romans 3:21–4:25. These verses seem clearly intended as an elaboration of the opening statement in 1:16–17.[41] They repeat the opening reference to God's righteousness and refer, as before, to its revelation or disclosure.[42] They also elaborate on the theme of faith that was introduced so enigmatically in 1:17. The only major term of 1:16–17 that is not explicitly repeated in these verses is "salvation," but Paul does refer to "redemption," a nearly synonymous term that evokes the memory of God's earlier redemptions (lit. "buying back") of Israel from slavery in Egypt and Babylon.[43] There are also several references to "justification," and Paul later explains that those who are justified will surely be saved (5:9–10). So though the word is absent, the concept of salvation is abundantly conveyed. Paul is not, however, simply repeating at greater length what he said earlier. He is now contrasting this new revelation of God's righteousness with the way that righteousness has been experienced in the past, that is, with the righteousness of God as it was depicted in 1:18–3:20.[44]

The major point of contrast is that now God's righteousness has been revealed "apart from law." This has at least two implications. First, it implies that God's righteousness will not be experienced as legal (that is, law-based) justice. Paul develops this point is 3:24: "They are now justi-fied *by his grace as a gift*." Second, it implies that God's righteousness will not be experienced exclusively or primarily as an act of deliverance for the people of the law, that is, the people of the law-based covenant. Paul devel-ops this point in verses 22b–23 and again in verses 29–30: "The righteous-ness of God [is] . . . for *all* who believe. For there is no distinction, since *all* have sinned and fall short of the glory of God. . . . Or is God the God of Jews only? Is he not the God of Gentiles also? Yes, of Gentiles also, since God is one."

The disclosure of God's righteousness is not simply apart from law. It is more positively described as through *pisteōs Iēsou Christou*. The mean-ing of this assertion is, however, anything but clear. The first problem is that the Greek phrase can be rendered either "through faith in Jesus Christ" or "through the faithfulness of Jesus Christ." The issue is strongly disputed, but for reasons developed in chapter 3, I think the lat-ter is the better translation. The second problem is that Paul supplies no verb to clarify the connection between "the righteousness of God" and "the faithfulness of Jesus Christ." The two phrases simply stand next to each other in the text. Various verbs have been proposed,[45] but if Paul followed customary Greek conventions, it is most likely that he intended for the reader to supply the verb that appeared in the first half of the verse: "But now, apart from law, the righteousness of God *has been dis-closed*, . . . the righteousness of God [*has been disclosed*] through the faith-fulness of Jesus Christ."[46] Even if this is the correct understanding of the text—and clearly not all agree that it is—it is not immediately obvious how *God's* righteousness has been revealed through *Jesus'* faithfulness. Paul attempts to explain.

If Paul's statement is interpreted in the simplest and most straightfor-ward way, it asserts that Jesus' faithfulness—his utter faithfulness to God—mirrors, and by doing so reveals, God's utter faithfulness, that is, God's righteousness.[47] This interpretation, though powerful in its direct-ness, defines *God's* righteousness through *Jesus'* actions. Paul shifts the dis-cussion to how God's righteousness is revealed through what *God* has done: "They are now justified by his grace as a gift, through the redemp-tion that is in Jesus Christ, whom God put forward as a sacrifice of atone-ment by his blood, effective through faith. *He did this to show his righteousness* because in his divine forbearance he had passed over the sins previously committed" (vv. 24–25). God, Paul says, showed God's righ-teousness by putting forward, that is, by establishing or regarding, Jesus' death as a sacrifice of atonement made effective as such by Jesus' faithfulness.[48] The final words of verse 25 underline that this "putting forward" of Jesus' death as an atoning sacrifice was a manifestation of God's righteousness precisely because it dealt with the sins that God had previously passed over.[49] That is, in God's act of salvation sins have not been simply ignored (which would not be right or fitting). They have been dealt with in a way consistent with God's righteousness. Here notions of divine justice seem to predominate: God's act of free redemption did not overturn or abandon God's righteous justice.

Paul makes one more attempt in verse 26 to explain how Jesus' faithful death shows God's righteousness: "It was to prove[50] at the present time that he himself is righteous and that he justifies the one who has the faith of Jesus" (NRSV, following the reading in the textual note). This assertion can be interpreted in two ways. First, by drawing on the assertion that Jesus' death was an effective sacrifice of atonement, Paul could be emphasizing again that with such a sacrifice dealing with sin God can continue to justify (declare righteous) those who have faith (but who have not done the "deeds prescribed by law") without impugning God's own righteous justice.[51]

A second possibility is that Paul is here anticipating the emphasis he will soon place on participation in Christ (6:1–14; 8:1–17). In this case Paul is asserting that God is righteous *in that* God is justifying (declaring righteous) the one who has, by virtue of participation in Christ, gained Christ's own faithfulness.[52] (Please see chapter 3 for the necessary background for this interpretation.) Here again Paul shows a concern to defend the rightness or justice of God's act of declaring righteous not just anyone, but the one who possesses (by virtue of participation in Christ) the faithfulness that Christ displayed. But the emphasis is now on God's positive act of declaring persons righteous, not the more passive "passing over" of their former sins.[53] That is, God's righteousness is here identified more closely as God's active saving righteousness rather than God's concern to maintain righteous standards of justice. The climax of the passage (3:27–30) lists the result of the redemption that is in Christ Jesus: boasting—that is, Jewish boasting in their privileged status as God's covenant people[54]—is excluded because right standing before God is available to both Jews and Gentiles alike.

In this important passage Paul clearly links this disclosure of God's righteousness with the death of Jesus, yet he does not pursue a single line of interpretation. Jesus' death is interpreted as an act of faithfulness, a means of redemption, and an atoning sacrifice; and God's righteousness is linked with this event in different ways. No line of interpretation is fully or clearly developed, and nuances of God's righteous justice, faithfulness, and saving activity are all present. What is clear is the emphasis on the fact that Jesus' death is a disclosure of God's righteousness; that through it God's saving righteousness extends equally and impartially to Jews and Gentiles alike; and that God's righteous justice has not been undermined. Oddly, there are few overtones of covenant faithfulness. Indeed, some pointed questions reveal the extent to which that concept has been challenged: "Is God the God of Jews only? Is he not the God of Gentiles also?" (v. 29).

There are no references to God's righteousness in chapter 4, nor are there any references to the covenant between God and Israel. There are, however, repeated references to God's promises to Abraham, in particular the promises that he and his offspring would inherit the world (4:13)[55] and that his offspring would include many nations (v. 17)—that is, Gentiles as well as Jews. The emphasis on Abraham's utter trust in the God who gave the promises evokes the image of the utterly trustworthy God. Here then is the direction that Paul takes the notion of God's faithfulness at this point in the argument: not God's faithfulness to the covenant with Israel at Sinai but God's faithfulness to the promises to Abraham that his offspring, those who would inherit the world, would include both Jews and Gentiles. The ambiguous *logia* of 3:2 seems to be belatedly defined in this chapter as the promises to Abraham. Through Christ and in Christ these promises are now being fulfilled (4:23–25).[56]

Romans 10:1–4. After the exposition of 3:21–4:25, Paul continues in subsequent chapters to explore issues more or less directly related to God's righteousness.[57] He does not, however, *mention* the concept again until chapter 10, and when he finally does so, it is in a passage filled with perplexities.

> Brothers and sisters, my heart's desire and prayer to God for them [Israel] is that they may be saved. I can testify that they have a zeal for God, but it is not enlightened [lit. "according to discernment"]. For, being ignorant of the righteousness of God,[58] and seeking to establish their own [righteousness], they have not submitted to God's righteousness. For Christ is the end [or "goal," the Greek word has both meanings] of the law so that there may be righteousness for everyone who believes. (10:1–4 NRSV, alt.)

The key to unlocking the meaning of this passage is resolving the nature of the contrast Paul is establishing between right and wrong understandings of God's righteousness. Two quite different proposals have been made. According to one, the contrast is between *seeking to establish* (that is, to earn) one's own righteousness and *receiving* the righteousness that comes from God as a gift. That is, the passage contrasts the works-righteousness characteristic of the Jews with the gift-righteousness that comes through Christ. Though this interpretation is encouraged by the references to "striving for righteousness" in the previous verses (9:30–33), and though a number of scholars argue strongly for it,[59] there are difficulties. Not the least of these is the problematic assumption that works-righteousness was characteristic of first-century Judaism and was the focus of Paul's concern. (Please see chapter 2 for a full discussion of this issue.)

According to the second proposal, the intended contrast is between a Jewish desire to establish (that is, to confirm) the righteousness that was exclusively (or distinctively) theirs through observance of the law, and submission to the radical nature of God's righteousness revealed through the gospel, a righteousness that extends salvation to all who believe, Jews and Gentiles alike.[60] That is, the passage contrasts seeking to confirm *Jewish* access to saving righteousness with conceding the *universal* dimensions of God's righteousness.

The passage is difficult, with some aspects of it lending support to one line of interpretation and other aspects supporting the other. The wider context is, however, decisively in favor of the second proposal. These verses appear at the very heart of a section of the letter (Rom 9–11) devoted to demonstrating two things: (1) that God has not abandoned God's covenant people, Israel, or the covenant itself (see esp. 9:4–5; 11:1, 11–12, 29), and (2) that God's people now includes Gentiles as well as Jews (see esp. 9:6–8, 22–24; 10:11–13; 11:25–32). In this setting, rejecting a concept of righteousness of limited application and benefit and insisting on a concept of God's righteousness that includes everyone who believes make perfect sense. Indeed, the whole discussion of God's righteousness in this letter has been moving toward this conclusion.

Conclusion

Bultmann's definition of *dikaiosynē theou* in Paul's letters as God's gift of righteousness, oriented around individual appropriation of the gift, was rightly corrected by Käsemann, who insisted that Paul also intended the phrase to refer to God's own righteousness. This he understood not as a divine attribute but as divine activity, a manifestation of divine power.

Williams countered that it was, in fact, an *attribute* of God, but one that was known through the deeds of God. Käsemann had recognized that "God's righteousness" also contained the notion of divine faithfulness, but he claimed that this was the faithfulness of the Creator to all creation, not God's covenant faithfulness toward Israel. Today, though, covenant faithfulness figures prominently in definitions. The review of Paul's references to *dikaiosynē theou* in Romans suggests, however, that this current consensus may be in need of correction.

Paul is certainly in dialogue with the understanding that God's righteousness is appropriately manifested in covenant faithfulness, but his goal is to demonstrate that God's righteousness extends salvation to those not included among the covenant people, that is, to Gentiles who do not live under the law. Thus we have seen that following his initial statement that God's righteousness is manifested in the salvation now available to everyone who believes, Jew and Gentile alike, Paul explores the depth and breadth of God's righteous (that is, distributive) justice. He pushes this concept to a radical conclusion—Jews and Gentiles fare exactly the same before God's just tribunal—and uses that to ground the equally radical claim that Jews and Gentiles fare exactly the same in the gracious act of salvation that God has put forward in Christ. Nuances of righteous justice, covenant faithfulness, and faithfulness to the promises to Abraham all interact as Paul moves toward the conclusion that God's righteousness demands the salvation of both Jews and Gentiles and is therefore manifested in this salvation. In the final chapters of his exposition, Paul vigorously affirms God's covenant faithfulness to Israel, but he uses the concept of God's righteousness to challenge constrictive definitions of the beneficiaries of that faithfulness.

Is it possible to give a summary statement of Paul's understanding of *dikaiosynē theou*? Paul is convinced that God's righteousness is revealed in God's constancy, consistency, dependability, trustworthiness, and faithfulness. Sometimes he emphasizes God's consistent righteous justice; sometimes he emphasizes God's trustworthiness in fulfilling the promises to Abraham; and sometimes he emphasizes God's faithfulness to Israel. Paul's argument is inexorably moving toward the conclusion that God's righteousness is now active in Christ to include Gentiles in salvation, but along the way it "means" a number of things.

But why does Paul develop this concept in this direction only in this letter? As Paul understood the concept, it was intimately connected with the acceptance of Gentiles into the people of God. There are only two letters in the extant Pauline corpus where this is the prevailing concern.

Galatians is a very polemical letter. Paul is arguing vigorously and passionately against the message of his opponents, and their argument has, to a large degree, set the agenda for his response. They do not seem to have drawn on the concept of God's righteousness to defend their position, and therefore Paul does not refer to it either.

In Romans, however, the situation is different. Paul is not engaged in a debate with opponents, but is instead formulating his understanding of the gospel (as the power of God for salvation to everyone who believes) on his own theological terms. Although the letter is addressed to a predominantly Gentile church in Rome (1:13–15), and though Paul may have been concerned to address some tensions within that church (Rom 12–15), he probably had his upcoming defense of his law-free gospel before the still-skeptical leaders of the Jerusalem church also in mind (15:22–33).[61] He grounded the presentation of his gospel in a conviction these leaders could affirm: God's righteous justice falls equally upon all. From that he argued that God's saving righteousness must also be equally available to all; but at the same time he insisted that God's covenant faithfulness to Israel never falters. It was a brilliant piece of rhetoric and a breathtaking theological vision.

EXCURSUS: JUSTIFICATION

What excuse is there for relegating justification—surely the center of Paul's theology—to a mere excursus? I offer a few explanations.

First, it is not clear that justification (by faith) *is* the center of Paul's theology. It was most assuredly the theological heart of the Reformation and the consequent center of most Protestant denominations; and it is the center of most of the various Pauline theologies that scholars have constructed out of his writings. But its status in Paul's *own* theology or thought is much more ambiguous. The key word that Paul uses in discussing it— the verb "justify" (Greek *dikaioun*)—appears primarily in Romans (15 times) and Galatians (8 times). It occurs twice in 1 Corinthians, but only once with any theological import (6:11). Even in that verse (apparently a liturgical fragment) there is no association with grace and faith, crucial elements in Paul's discussions. Paul alludes to the concept in Phil 3:9 when he refers to the righteousness that comes from God, and perhaps again in 1 Cor 1:30 and 2 Cor 5:21 (see p. 49 above), but even with these additions one cannot say that justification is pervasive throughout the Pauline corpus. It certainly appears to be at the center of Paul's theological arguments in Romans and Galatians, but its absence, or near absence, in the rest of the letters lends some credibility to Albert Schweitzer's assessment that it was a "subsidiary crater" in Paul's thought.[62]

Not all, of course, agree. Some, like Nils Dahl, concede that the vocabulary of justification is missing from most of Paul's letters but attempt to demonstrate that the underlying idea informs Paul's arguments throughout.[63] Others base their objections on doctrinal grounds: if justification by faith is not the center, the foundation of Protestant Christianity is destroyed.[64] The status of justification in Paul's thought is ultimately unrecoverable; that it came to clear and consistent expression in only two letters is undeniable. What that says about the centrality of the concept to Paul continues to be debated.

Second, Paul's concept of justification is intimately related to his understanding of the righteousness of God: indeed, some lines of interpretation *equate* God's righteousness with justification. In the process of exploring the topic of "God's righteousness," the topic of justification has thus been, at least in part, addressed.

Third, Paul's concept of justification is also intrinsically linked to his concepts of grace and faith, and to his objection to works of the law. All of these topics are treated at some length in other essays in this volume, and all of those essays have necessarily included comments on justification. To provide a fulsome treatment here would thus be redundant in many ways. It would also be very difficult, for interpretations of these other components vary, and the different variations color the concept of justification in different ways, as the essays try to make clear. All that is needed and possible here is a discussion of the basic contours of justification, and that can be dealt with in a few pages.

Justification

English translations of the Bible obscure the relationship of the verb "justify" (*dikaioun*) to the noun "righteousness" (*dikaiosynē*) and to the adjective *dikaios* (variously translated "righteous" or "just"). This is unfortunate, for those connections establish the meaning of the verb: to "justify" persons is to make or pronounce them to be "righteous" or "in the right." In Paul's letters, of course, God is the one who justifies, and traditionally forensic or legal metaphors have been used to explain the action. God in the role of judge pronounces a verdict of acquittal on a guilty (sinful) defendant; that is, in anticipation of the final judgment God pronounces that person to be "righteous" (Rom 4:5). This forensic emphasis lies behind the Catholic-Protestant disputes over whether this was imputed righteousness, in which only the person's *status* before God was changed (the Protestant view), or an imparted righteousness, which involved actual moral *transformation* (the Catholic view).

More recent discussions of justification have emphasized the covenantal overtones of the concept. In the context of a covenant, to be righteous means to be in right relation to the other covenant members, to have fulfilled one's covenant obligations. Viewed from this perspective, in justifying persons God acts in the role of (dominant) covenant partner and establishes them in right relation to Godself. Since a relationship, especially a right relationship with God, has transformative power, traditional distinctions between imputed or imparted righteousness lose their relevance.[65] In addition, locating justification within a covenantal framework keeps the covenant community in view (a community that, in Paul's view, now included Gentiles) and prevents the concept from becoming purely individualistic.

Crucial to Paul's understanding, of course, is that this relationship is declared whole (or this acquittal is pronounced) by God's free, unmerited act ("by God's grace as a gift," Rom 3:24), unrelated to any "works of the law" (3:28). The recipients of the verdict or covenant status must, however, respond in faith or trust. I explore these issues in separate essays. The relationship between "justification" and "salvation," however, needs to be clarified. Paul does this (and more) in Rom 5:1–11:

> Therefore, since we are justified by faith, we have peace with God through our Lord Jesus Christ, through whom we have obtained access to this grace in which we stand; and we boast in our hope of sharing the glory of God. . . . And hope does not disappoint us, because God's love has been poured into our hearts through the Holy Spirit that has been given to us. For while we were still weak, at the right time Christ died for the ungodly. . . . But God proves his love for us in that while we still were sinners Christ died for us. Much more surely then, now that we have been justified by his blood, will we be saved through him from the wrath of God. For if while we were enemies, we were reconciled to God through the death of his Son, much more surely, having been reconciled, will we be saved by his life. But more than that, we even boast in God through our Lord Jesus Christ, through whom we have now received reconciliation.

In this important passage Paul describes the consequences of justification. Though once weak, ungodly sinners and enemies of God, those who have been justified have been reconciled to God. They are thus now in a relationship of peace with God (free of enmity and in a relationship of wholeness); they have also obtained access to God's favor and currently stand in it;[66] and they have been given the Holy Spirit both as the sign of their new status as beloved children of God (8:14–17) and as the power that enables them to please God (8:5–8). They are, however, not yet "saved." Paul used this word to refer to the eschatological climax, the end result of their justification, the final ascent to glory. *Now* they are justified; *then*—at the coming of Christ in glory, at the *final* judgment—they will be saved.[67] This salvation rests on justification (a right relationship with God), and because they have been justified, the hope of that final fulfillment will not be disappointed. Yet it remains, for the moment, "hope," and it is in that in-between state of having been justified and awaiting the future fulfillment of the hope of salvation that one lives out, and out of, the gift of a right relationship with God.

To end this essay with Rom 5 would create the wrong impression—that Paul's goal in developing his theology of justification was to explain how sinful individuals found peace and salvation with God. For many centuries that was understood to be Paul's goal, but that understanding ignored the content and context of the letters in which Paul developed his theology. Paul's concern in Galatians and Romans was with how Gentiles are to be included in the messianic community, and it was with *this* in mind that he formulated his theology of justification.[68] It is fitting, then, to end with a quotation that reminds us of this purpose:

> Or is God the God of Jews only? Is he not the God of Gentiles also? Yes, of Gentiles also, since God is one; and he will justify the circumcised on the ground of faith and the uncircumcised through that same faith. (Rom 3:29–30)

Chapter Six

The Future of "Israel"

Who Is Israel?

The future of Israel was an issue close to Paul's heart, and he could be passionate in discussing it. It is also an issue about which contemporary interpreters of Paul have strong passions. Add to that the fact that Paul, in his passion, did not write about the topic with utmost clarity, and we have the foundation for the current state of affairs: radically disparate assessments of the issue that are passionately defended by scholars appealing to the same set of texts but interpreting them in very different ways.

There is no prospect of a consensus view. All that can be done is to survey the evidence and discuss the options. At almost every point in the analysis one will face decisions that affect the outcome. One of the first is whether to assume that Paul's views remained consistent or to allow for the possibility that they changed over time. Theoretically one would decide this after looking at the evidence, but deep-seated convictions about inspiration often suggest the answer beforehand. If one does decide beforehand that Paul was fundamentally consistent, one must find some way to harmonize *apparently* different assertions, and that usually means allowing one passage to control the meaning. But which one?

A second decision that must be made fairly early in the process concerns which passages should count as evidence. Definitions are important here. The topic concerns "Israel," the people of God. It is not focused on "Judaism" as a pattern of religion or on the Jew as defined by circumcision and the law, important topics in their own right. Rather, it is focused on Israel "as chosen by God, the children of Israel, descendants of the patriarch (Jacob/Israel) through whom the choice and election came."[1] In short, the concern is with "Israel" defined primarily by its relationship to God. The question that Paul's writings raise is whether he thought that followers of Messiah Jesus had supplanted "Israel according to the flesh"—that is, Israel as an ethnic group—as the people of God. Should that prove to be the case, and I do not wish to prejudge the outcome of this investigation, it would not mean that in Paul's view Christianity had superseded Judaism, that is, that one religion had supplanted another. Christianity and Judaism were not at that time separate religions. It would mean that one Jewish sect (a sect that included uncircumcised Gentiles) claimed for itself the historically and theologically charged title "Israel" and denied that title to other Jews—much like the sectaries at Qumran did (though without the added factor of Gentile participation).[2] A second question then follows immediately: if this is the case, what future did Paul envision for the former "Israel"?

These comments indicate, I hope, what is at stake here. Even to raise the possibility that "Israel" is no longer ethnic Israel also raises a deeper question about God: Is God faithful to God's covenants (that is, God's covenants with ethnic Israel) or not? And to explore Paul's view of the future of ethnic Israel means encountering the possibility that he came to understand that God works salvation in mysterious—and different—ways. But that is the end of the story; we need to start at the beginning.

1 Thessalonians 2:14–16

Paul wrote this letter out of a deep sense of gratitude—and relief—that the Thessalonians had survived severe persecution with their faith intact. In the midst of his thanks to God for their abiding faith, however, comes this surprising outburst in the second chapter:

> [14]For you, brothers and sisters, became imitators of the churches of God in Christ Jesus that are in Judea, for you suffered the same things from your own compatriots as they did from the Jews, [15]who killed both the Lord Jesus and the prophets, and drove us out; they displease God and oppose everyone [16]by hindering us from speaking to the Gentiles so that they may be saved. Thus they have constantly been filling up the measure of their sins; but God's wrath has overtaken them *at last*.[3]

Nils Dahl notes that this is "one of the strongest anti-Jewish statements in the New Testament," and Richard Bell concludes that here "Paul's view concerning Israel is bleak in the extreme."[4] Few, however, claim that these verses *define* Paul's view. Some have challenged the authenticity of the passage. The language, they note, is not typical of Paul, and the theologically embarrassing sentiment expressed here is utterly incompatible with that of Rom 9–11. Assuming then that Paul was reasonably consistent and that Romans represents his true convictions, they attribute these verses to a later scribe.[5] Others reject the assumption of consistency. They accept these verses as Paul's own words and acknowledge that they present a harsh and global condemnation of Israel. But, they argue, Paul's thinking on this subject changed.[6]

It is also argued that the verses do not proclaim a blanket condemnation of all Jews or an eternal one. By deleting the "antisemitic comma"[7] between verses 14 and 15, Paul's ire and condemnation are directed only toward those Jews who actively persecuted the Judean churches and hindered Paul's mission.[8] And by selecting a different translation for *eis telos*, one can argue that even for them God's wrath is only "until the end," at which point things might change (as Rom 11 indicates). In short, these verses are very problematic. They are open to a variety of interpretations; they may not be by Paul; and if they are from Paul's hand, they were obviously written in anger. Few are willing to ground Paul's view of Israel's future in this outburst.

Philippians 3:2–3

In Philippians 3 we find a similar outburst. After filling several chapters with expressions of his joy and equanimity even in the midst of opposition and persecution (1:12–26; 2:17–18; 3:1), Paul suddenly says: "Beware of the dogs, beware of the evil workers, beware of 'the mutilation'! For it is we who are the circumcision" (3:2 NRSV, following the textual note). The identity of the objects of this vicious attack is not clear.[9] The "dogs" could be Jews,[10] Jewish followers of Christ,[11] rival missionaries who insist on circumcision,[12] or even Gentile converts to Judaism.[13] This ambiguity imposes serious limitations on our ability to assess the significance of Paul's assertion that "[they are] the mutilation; *we* [the emphasis is strong in the Greek] are the circumcision." If those castigated as "dogs" are not Jews in general (and this seems to me most likely), then Paul is *not* claiming that Jews are now "the mutilation" and (by implication) no longer "the circumcision." He would be simply attacking a much more restricted group, most likely rival missionaries. But if "dogs" refers to Jews, he *is* making that claim, and in so doing he is rather far along the way toward a notion of supersession.[14] Only the appropriation of the name "Israel" is missing.

1 Corinthians 10

It is only out of excessive scholarly zeal that 1 Cor 10 is sometimes cited as evidence of Paul's negative view of the future of Israel.[15] Verses 1–11 mention instances of past punishments of Israel as a warning to the Gentile believers of Corinth. They do not report or predict the eschatological demise of Israel. Furthermore, the reference to "Israel according to the flesh" in verse 18 (NRSV: "the people of Israel") is not, in this context, negative, just as the reference to the "new covenant" in 11:25 does not, by itself, imply the annulment of the old.[16] Without a contrasting reference to "Israel according to the promise" or "Israel according to the Spirit"—and there is none here—it does not carry implications of supersession or condemnation. "According to the flesh" is used in a neutral sense, as occasionally elsewhere in Paul's letters (e.g., Rom 1:3; 4:1; 9:3, 5). Here it designates ethnic Israel (as conveyed by the NRSV and NJB translations) or Israel with all its customs (REB: "consider Jewish practice").[17]

Some translations foster the notion of a condemnation of Israel by rendering verse 20 as "I mean that what they [*the Jews*] sacrifice, [they sacrifice] to demons and not to God" (NAB). Some ancient manuscripts contain this reading, but the evidence of the best of these manuscripts supports the reading given by most translations: "What *pagans* sacrifice, they sacrifice to demons and not to God" (NRSV, REB, NJB). If one does not read preconceptions into this letter, 1 Corinthians is mute on the question of the future of Israel. Second Corinthians, however, is not so mute.

2 Corinthians 3

The situation Paul is addressing in this letter is the arrival in Corinth of rival missionaries, who have apparently stolen the hearts, minds, and allegiance of the Corinthians.[18] Paul struggles to reclaim the church to his understanding of the gospel, at times going on the attack against his rivals, at times defending himself against their accusations, but most of the time doing both simultaneously. This portion of the letter is one of those times: "For we are not peddlers of God's word *like so many*" (2:17); "Surely we do not need, *as some do*, letters of recommendation to you or from you, do we?" (3:1). After presenting himself as a competent minister of a new, life-giving covenant (3:5–6), Paul launches into an argument that is distinct enough from the surrounding material that some regard it as a digression. It has, however, too many points of contact with the surrounding "apologetic polemics" to be a real digression.[19] Indeed, it continues Paul's attack on his rivals, but in a different, midrashic mode.

At first Paul stays relatively on target. Without explicitly mentioning the rival ministers, he launches into a description of a ministry of death (v. 7) and condemnation (v. 9) that can only be an allusion to their ministry. He grants the glory of this ministry, but, he says, that glory is being set aside (v. 11), supplanted by the greater glory of the ministry of justification (that is, by Paul's ministry). Thus far the brunt of Paul's attack falls on his rivals, but in verse 12 he broadens its scope to include not simply the rival missionaries in Corinth, but also the Mosaic covenant itself and all those who are under it. In a very free interpretation of Exod 34, Paul contrasts his ministry with that of Moses:

> We act with great boldness, not like Moses, who put a veil over his face to keep the people of Israel from gazing at the end of what was being set aside. But their minds were hardened. Indeed, to this very day, when they hear the reading of the old covenant, that same veil is still there, since only in Christ is it set aside. Indeed, to this very day whenever Moses is read, a veil lies over their minds; but when one turns to the Lord, the veil is removed. (2 Cor 3:12b–16)

The whole passage (2:17–3:18) bristles with difficulties. Paul's metaphors are very fluid, with "veil" and "glory" rather confusingly used with reference to a variety of things. Moreover, Paul is clearly appropriating the language of his rivals and turning the accusations *they* have leveled against *him* back upon *them* (see, e.g., 4:3). It is impossible, however, to know how far this appropriation extends and how much our interpretation would change if we could "hear" more clearly the echoes of his opponents' words.[20] Even with these considerations, though, it is difficult to deny that Paul is close to articulating something like a doctrine of supersession.[21] What Moses brought is an "old covenant"—the first and only time this phrase appears in the New Testament—and that covenant, not just the rival ministry to bring the Gentile converts of Corinth under that covenant, is what is being set aside.[22] To be sure, says Paul, "Moses" is still being read, but "Moses" is understood only "when one turns to the Lord," that is, when one accepts the gospel of Christ.[23]

Galatians 4:21–31; 6:16

Galatians is certainly the most polemical, and in many ways the most problematic, of Paul's letters. Rival teachers or missionaries had come to Galatia and were attempting—with obvious success—to persuade Paul's Gentile converts there that they had to confirm their faith with circumcision. Faith, they said, was important but inadequate. To become part of the people of God one must have (that is, *men* must have) the sign of God's covenant in their flesh, and all must live according to the requirements of God's covenant law. In his letter Paul attacks these people and their motives and presents a vigorous refutation of their message. Two portions of his rebuttal seem to touch directly on the subject of the future of Israel: the allegory of 4:21–31 and the closing benediction in 6:16.

Galatians 4:21–31. There is widespread agreement that Paul's choice of Gen 16 and 21 as the basis for his argument was dictated by the rival missionaries. They were probably using the story of Isaac and Ishmael recounted there to support their insistence on circumcision (see Gen 17:23–27; 21:4); Paul, however, takes the story in a different direction. First he summarizes the text, with some interpretive additions:[24] two women (slave and free), two sons (one born "according to the flesh," the other "through the promise"). He then pronounces this story to be an allegory (Gal 4:24; Greek *allēgoroumena*), that is, it refers to something other than its literal meaning.

Allegories are notoriously flexible, open to a multitude of interpretations unless the author directs the way. Paul does. The two women, he says, are two covenants. Hagar (who bears children for slavery) is from Mount Sinai and corresponds to "the present Jerusalem." Sarah (not mentioned by name, but identified as "our" mother) corresponds to "the Jerusalem above." Paul also provides the application: the Galatians are children of the promise, like Isaac; and just as Isaac was persecuted by Ishmael, so too are the Galatian believers being persecuted, presumably by the children of Hagar. Scripture, he says, provides the remedy: "Drive out the slave and her child; for the child of the slave will not share the inheritance with the child of the free woman" (v. 30, citing Gen 21:10).

The key to deciphering the allegory is the link between Hagar, Sinai (where God gave the law and established the covenant with Israel), and present Jerusalem. In a stunning and audacious reversal of the text, Paul equates the Hagar-Ishmael line with Judaism and the Sarah-Isaac line with those who believe in Christ. These believers have replaced Israel as the legitimate children of Abraham, and with the command to "drive out the slave and her child" Paul declares that "all Jews who do not believe in Christ are to be cast out, . . . unbelieving Jews are rejected by God, . . . [and] it can even be inferred that Paul is bringing Judaism to an end."[25] This seems a fairly straightforward reading, and it has many adherents. J. Louis Martyn, however, insists that it is wrong, and he too has a number of adherents. His argument is as follows.

Almost without exception, when Paul refers elsewhere to Jerusalem, he has the Jerusalem church, that is, the community of believers in Jerusalem, in mind, not Judaism per se.[26] In the references to "bearing children" (vv. 23 and 29), Paul replaces the verb in the Genesis story that refers to the woman's act of birthing (Greek *tiktein*) with another verb (*gennan*) that can refer to the man's act of begetting and that elsewhere in his letters refers to the missionary activity of creating individual believers and Gentile churches (Phlm 10; 1 Cor 4:14–15; Gal 4:31).[27] Finally (and decisively), Martyn insists that Paul's overriding concern throughout this letter is with his opponents, who seem to be linked to, and perhaps sponsored by, the Jerusalem church[28] and who are seeking to impose circumcision and law observance on his Gentile converts. Thus, Martyn concludes, Hagar represents the rival missionaries (not Judaism), and her offspring are those Galatian converts who have embraced their teachings. Paul's emphatic conclusion is, "Cast out these missionaries and their followers."[29] There is, on this reading, no rejection of Judaism per se.

Galatians 6:16. Paul closes his letter with an unusual benediction: "As for those who follow this rule [that is, the rule that circumcision does not matter, that "new creation" in Christ is all that matters; v. 15]—peace be upon them, and mercy, and upon the Israel of God." Who is this "Israel of God"? Does it refer to ethnic Israel or to some portion of ethnic Israel? Or is Paul transferring to the church this ancient and significant name?

The verse is utterly ambiguous. As translated above, "those who follow this rule" and "the Israel of God" seem to be two different groups. The verse can, however, with equal justification be translated in a way that equates the two groups: "All who take this principle for their guide, peace and mercy be upon them, the Israel of God" (REB).[30] If the second translation is correct, the Israel of God is the community of believing Jews and Gentiles. Both Richard Bell and J. Louis Martyn follow this interpretation but draw different conclusions regarding Paul's intent. Bell sees a substitution model here: "The Church of Jews and Gentiles replaces Israel as the people of God."[31] Martyn, however, says that Paul was not thinking of the Jewish people when he wrote this. He was focused tightly on the situation in Galatia and was countering the way his opponents were using the name "Israel." "It would be a great mistake to attribute to Paul the simplistic view that the church has replaced the Jewish people as God's own."[32]

What if the first translation is correct? In that case there are a number of interpretive options: (1) Those walking according to the rule are Gentile believers; the "Israel of God" designates Jewish believers. (2) Those walking according to the rule are all current believers, both Jews and Gentiles; the "Israel of God" designates those within Israel who will, in the future, accept the gospel.[33] (3) The "Israel of God" is all Israel, the same group referred to in Rom 11:26.[34] (4) The "Israel of God" is "the Israel of God's future—not the Judaism of Paul's day but Israel made complete by the inclusion of all nations [that is, Gentiles], in accordance with God's promise to Abraham (Gal 3:8)."[35] Options one and two imply that the part of Israel that does not accept the gospel is no longer "of God." Option four affirms the status of ethnic Israel before God but also envisions Gentiles being incorporated into this entity. Option three is discussed below.

In short, this enigmatic statement does not reveal Paul's view of the future of Israel, at least not to us. Quite the contrary, almost any understanding of Paul's view of that future can be, and has been, read into it. By and large, the way one interprets the allegory of Galatians 4, itself enigmatic, is decisive here. If Hagar represents Judaism, then the church, or some portion of it, is the Israel of God. If she represents only the rival missionaries, other options are possible. So has the church supplanted Israel in Paul's view? Galatians gives no unambiguous answer.

And so we come to Romans.

Romans 9–11

Paul wrote to the Roman churches without the provocation of rival missionaries. In fact, he wrote without much provocation at all, for he had never visited this city. There seem to have been tensions in the churches there, perhaps between Jewish and Gentile believers (Rom 14–15); indeed, the Gentile believers seem to have developed an arrogant attitude that Paul was concerned to correct (11:13–24). Paul was also worried about an upcoming trip to Jerusalem and the response of the church leaders there to his ministry to the Gentiles (15:30–32), even as he was planning a trip to continue that ministry in Spain (15:22–24).

With these things on his mind, the thematic focus of the letter is that God's righteousness has been revealed to include Jews *and* Gentiles in salvation (1:16–17). In the course of developing this theme, Paul makes some assertions that call into question Israel's special status with God. The Jewish law, the foundation of Israel's covenant with God, provides no advantage (2:12–16). Circumcision, the sign of the covenant, is strictly a matter of the heart (2:25–29). And the name of God has been blasphemed—a truly serious charge—among the Gentiles because of some Jews (2:17–24). Paul articulates the questions that this line of argument raises: "What advantage has the Jew?" (3:1). "What if some [Jews] were unfaithful? Will their faithlessness nullify the faithfulness of God?" (3:3). Initially he gives brief but emphatic answers to these questions ("Much, in every way" and "By no means!" respectively), but he returns to the issue at greater length in chapters 9–11.

By that point in the argument more was at stake than God's faithfulness to Israel. Paul had just recounted God's words of promise to believers (see esp. 8:18–39), but if God's word of promise to Israel has failed, what confidence can now be placed in these new promises? Paul was compelled by his argument to defend his assertion that God's faithfulness to Israel has not failed (9:6). But he was also compelled by family bonds to defend this assertion: these were his own people, his kindred according to the flesh (9:3). His defense involved probing the future and the very identity of Israel.[36] His argument is complex (some would say convoluted and contradictory), often emotional, and far too lengthy to treat in its entirety here. I will review his opening comments in chapter 9 and then focus on chapter 11, where the question of Israel's identity and future comes to a head.

The remnant and the rest. Paul opens this portion of the letter by passionately expressing his anguish over Israel, whom he has earlier described as "unfaithful" (3:3). He continues by listing the rich religious heritage that their faithlessness has apparently jeopardized: the adoption, the glory, the covenants, the law, the worship, the promises, the patriarchs, and, of course, the Messiah. He then reasserts what he stated earlier: "It is not as though the word of God [that is, the promises of God] had failed" (9:6; cf. 3:4). Now, though, he explains why that is so: "Not all those from Israel are 'Israel'" (AT). Here Paul draws on the biblical concept of the remnant (see Isa 10:20–23; Mic 5:7–8) to argue that God's word of promise will be fulfilled with a *portion* of Israel who now *are* "Israel." These are chosen by God's mysterious election grace, the arbitrariness of which is both emphasized ("So then he has mercy on whomever he chooses, and he hardens the heart of whomever he chooses," Rom 9:18) and defended in the rest of the chapter with scriptural images and quotations. Those who are not chosen are not counted as true descendants of Abraham or children of God.

As Paul begins to draw the argument of chapters 9–11 to a close, he restates as a question the assertion with which he began: "I ask, then, has God rejected his people?" (11:1; cf. 9:6). As in chapter 9, he defends his emphatic negative reply ("By no means!") by drawing on the concept of the remnant: God's faithfulness to the people of Israel is confirmed by the continuing existence of a faithful group within Israel, "a remnant [Greek *leimma*] chosen by grace." Paul proves the existence of this group by pointing to himself and by providing a biblical proof text. Then he summarizes the situation as he sees it: "What then? Israel failed to obtain what it was seeking." One group within Israel, characterized by election, "obtained it."[37] "The rest" (Greek *hoi loipoi*), however, "were hardened" and presumably did not. In 9:6 Paul calls the first group (the elect) "Israel," effectively denying that name to the rest. In 11:7, however, "Israel" is either the name given to the rest ("'Israel' failed to obtain what it was seeking") or (more likely) "Israel" refers to Israel as a whole, *both* the remnant *and* the rest. Here "the rest," though hardened, remain a part of "Israel."[38]

Paul's initial focus is on the second group, "the rest." He provides two scriptural warrants for his claim that they were hardened, the first verifying that the hardening was by God (11:8). Through references here and in chapter 9 to God's hardening as the cause of Israel's failure, Paul undermines any ascription of blame to them for that failure. It was, mysteriously, due to God's own act. Moreover, the second scripture citation asserts that the hardening is "forever" (11:10). With scripture's voice so clear and authoritative, it is surprising that Paul immediately asks, "Have they stumbled so as to fall?" That is, is their situation permanent? Even more surprising is the answer Paul gives to his own question, "By no means!" Nothing Paul has said thus far prepares the reader for his explanation.

Paul explains that God's hardening of Israel and their consequent stumbling had a purpose—it allowed salvation to come to the Gentiles. Then, even more surprisingly, he states that the salvation of the Gentiles itself has a larger purpose—to make Israel envious and so to provoke them into salvation! Paul thus wonders aloud, "Now if their stumbling means riches for the world, and if their defeat means riches for Gentiles, how much more will their *full inclusion* mean?" (11:12). With this, the tenor of Paul's argument changes dramatically. He notes that by his own ministry he might save "some" (v. 14) and then returns to a variation of the concept of a remnant. This time he does not use it to distinguish the hardened "rest" from the saved remnant but to point to their shared essence: "If the part of the dough offered as first fruits [the remnant] is holy, then the *whole batch* [remnant and rest] *is holy*" (v. 16). He concludes this portion of his argument with a rather transparent allegory: branches ("the rest") were broken off an olive tree (Israel), and wild olive shoots (Gentiles) have been grafted in (vv. 17–22). The obvious purpose of the allegory is to use the example of "the rest" to warn Gentiles about the folly of arrogance: "Do not become proud, but stand in awe. For if God did not spare the natural branches, perhaps he will not spare you" (vv. 20–21).[39] Yet at the end Paul returns to the fate of "the rest": "For if you have been cut from what is by nature a wild olive tree and grafted, contrary to nature, into a cultivated olive tree, *how much more will these natural branches be grafted back into their own olive tree*" (v. 24).

The mystery. In verses 25–26a Paul shifts from telling an allegory to presenting a mystery: "So that you may not claim to be wiser than you are, brothers and sisters, I want you to understand [lit. I would not have you ignorant of] this mystery: a hardening has come upon part of Israel, until the full number of the Gentiles has come in. And so all Israel will be saved." What is the mystery that Paul unveils? With this language the reader expects a new revelation, so each part of Paul's subsequent statement needs careful attention.

"*A hardening has come upon part of Israel*": Paul has asserted this several times and discussed it at length in these chapters (9:6–24; 11:5–11).[40] It is not a new revelation.

"*until the full number of Gentiles has come in*": Paul has previously stated that the hardening is not permanent (vv. 11–12). What is new here is that he identifies the factor that determines the end of the hardening: the coming in, that is, the coming to faith, of the full number of Gentiles. The "full number" probably refers to the number of Gentiles that God intends to save, not to all Gentiles.[41] When that number has been reached, the hardening will end.

"*And so all Israel will be saved*": This is the climax of the passage, but who is "all Israel"? That is surely part of the mystery, and there are several possibilities.

1. "All Israel" is the elect of Israel. This could include not only the original remnant but also those in Israel who subsequently come to faith,[42] but there would still be a "rest" that remains outside "all Israel." This interpretation draws on the redefinition of Israel that Paul presented in 9:6 ("Not all those from Israel are Israel") and his citation of Isa 10:22–23 in Rom 9:27 ("Only a remnant of them will be saved"). It does not, however, take account of the way Paul has developed the argument since then or his emphasis here on *all* Israel.

2. "All Israel" is what has been called "spiritual Israel,"[43] the (relatively small) elect remnant plus the (much larger) "full number of Gentiles." This interpretation follows Paul's words in verse 25 very carefully. In this verse Paul refers (by implication) to an unhardened portion of Israel and to the full number of Gentiles; he does not allude to the regrafting of the natural branches ("the rest") mentioned in verses 23–24 or to the "full inclusion" of Israel mentioned in verse 12. Did he present them earlier as merely hypothetical possibilities? Does the mystery exclude them by silence? This line of interpretation assumes that it does. When the two groups mentioned here have been saved, by definition "all Israel" will have been saved. "Israel," on this interpretation, has no ethnic connotations. It is defined exclusively by faith and comprises primarily Gentiles but also a few Jews.

3. "All Israel" is all of Israel, the elect and the rest combined.[44] In addition to the full number of Gentiles, all of Israel will also be saved. According to this interpretation, which is strongly supported by verses 28–32 and widely accepted as Paul's most likely meaning, the mystery incorporates the full development of Paul's thought in this chapter, and "Israel" remains ethnic Israel.[45] But *how* will "all Israel" be saved? This seems to be part of the mystery too, and on this there is far less agreement.

By way of offering an explanation Paul quotes Isa 59:20–21:

> Out of Zion will come the deliverer;
>   he will banish ungodliness from Jacob.
> And this is my covenant with them,
>   when I take away their sins.
>   (Rom 11:26b–27)

It is typical of Paul that his citation is not exact. The Hebrew text of Isaiah refers to the deliverer coming "*to* Zion," and the Septuagint reads "*on account of* Zion," but Paul says the deliverer will come "*out of* Zion." The last line, "when I take away their sins," resembles nothing in Isa 59; it was probably drawn from Isa 27:9. But what does the passage, with these changes, actually mean? First, who is the deliverer? Second, how—that is, on what basis—will he save "the rest"?

According to some, the coming of the deliverer is a reference to the Parousia, the second coming of Christ. Several strong arguments are cited in support of this interpretation. In 1 Thess 1:10 Paul refers to Jesus at the Parousia as "the deliverer," using the same words (*ho rhyomenos*) found here.[46] Paul's alteration of the text of Isaiah to read "out of (heavenly) Zion" creates (it is argued) a clear and deliberate reference to the Parousia, when Jesus is expected to descend out of the heavenly Jerusalem (i.e., heavenly Zion) to deliver the elect (Gal 4:26; Heb 12:22; and Rev 3:12; 21:2).

Others, however, find significance in the lack of any explicit reference to Christ and assert that the deliverer must be God. Strong arguments are cited in support of this interpretation as well. The original text of Isaiah refers to God, and references to Christ have all but dropped out of Paul's argument.[47] Even the closing hymn and benediction (Rom 11:33–36) refer only to God, though elsewhere in similar passages Paul always includes references to Christ (Gal 1:3–5; Phil 4:19–20; 1 Cor 15:57; 2 Cor 1:3). When Paul uses the verb "deliver" (*rhyomai*, also translated "rescue") elsewhere in Romans, it seems to be God who acts as deliverer (Rom 7:24; 15:31; see also 2 Cor 1:10). The change that Paul made in the reference to Zion ("out of" instead of "to" or "on account of") was, according to this line of interpretation, intended to evoke the image of Zion (that is, *earthly* Jerusalem) as God's dwelling place, out of which God comes to save "the rest" (see, e.g., Pss 14:7; 53:6).

The deliverer, then, could be either God or Christ at the Parousia, with the evidence (and scholars) rather evenly divided. The more important question regarding Israel's future, however, is *how* the rest of Israel will be saved. The most frequent answer is that, regardless of the identity of the deliverer, they will be saved by their faith in Christ. Though this is not explicitly stated in this passage, throughout this letter Paul has insisted that justification (and thus salvation) is only through faith in Christ, and (it is argued) Paul could not and would not abandon that deepest conviction at this point in the letter.[48] The only difference, then, between the salvation of "the rest" at the Parousia and the earlier salvation of the remnant is the timing and the vehicle. They are brought to this faith not by the preaching of missionaries like Paul, but by a direct encounter with God or the risen Christ.

Others argue that if the salvation of "the rest" were by their coming to faith in Christ, Paul would surely have mentioned it, and he does not do so.[49] Instead, he mentions the covenant, and so this salvation will be by grace alone (as it is for Gentiles), but out of God's faithfulness to God's covenant with Israel. If Christ is the one who will appear as deliverer, "it is Christ in a different role," bringing salvation to Israel in a "special way" under its covenant with God.[50] Some insist that this was Paul's conviction all along; that from the beginning of his ministry Paul understood and preached Christ as God's way of salvation *for Gentiles*. Jews have always been, and continue to be, related to God through the covenant.[51] Others suggest that it reflects Paul's tactical decision not to be "off-putting" to Jews as he prepares to go to Jerusalem.[52] This line of argument implies an element of deception in the ambiguity of Paul's argument. Still others claim that Paul just came to this insight as he was writing the letter, that it represents a sudden and very dramatic change in his thought.[53]

What can we make of this? Paul's view of the future of Israel all comes down to this passage in Romans that resolutely resists a definitive interpretation. One can put the pieces of the argument together in a way that redefines "Israel" as all believers, Jews and Gentiles, and by implication denies that name—and salvation—to all Jews who have not accepted Christ. One can put the pieces together in a way that retains the name "Israel" only for ethnic Israel and affirms the salvation of ethnic Israel as a whole because all will turn to Christ. One can put the pieces together in a way that retains the name "Israel" for the descendants of Abraham and affirms their salvation on the basis of their covenant with God. Drawing on Galatians, one can add that Gentiles become part of this Israel, part of Abraham's offspring, by sharing the faith of Abraham (Rom 4:16; Gal 3:7), which is theirs when they belong to Christ (Gal 3:14, 29). This reverses the conclusion of the first option. There "Israel" is defined by faith in Christ, and Jews can become part of "Israel" if they have this faith. Here "Israel" is defined by descent from Abraham, and Gentiles can become part of "Israel" if they belong to Christ, the seed ("offspring") of Abraham. Many options: how does one decide?

The vague allusiveness of Paul's language allows—indeed, almost requires—the presuppositions of the reader to take charge of the interpretation.[54] Some interpreters are very clear about their presuppositions. Bell, for example, works from the convictions that "the view of the New Testament and in particular of Paul is that there is no salvation outside Jesus Christ," and that "Christian theology, if properly done, is going to be inevitably 'supersessionist.'"[55] Thus Bell can read Rom 11:27 only as a message of Israel's ultimate salvation through faith in Christ. To read it otherwise is "selling out" the Christian gospel.[56]

Gaston starts at a different point: "I write in the context of the second half of the twentieth century in the firm conviction that things which happened in the first half must mean a radical and irrevocable change in the way Christians do theology. . . . Very central [after Auschwitz] is the recognition that Judaism is a living reality and that the covenant between God and Israel continues." This conviction, he says, "should not inspire an apologetic revision of texts written in the past"; but "it can also open exegetical eyes and make it possible to see texts in a new way and perhaps understand them better."[57] These convictions open his eyes to the conclusion that "it would be completely wrong to speak [in reference to Rom 11:25–27] of an end-time conversion" to Christ.[58] Stendahl draws no such conclusion, but he does hear a clear directive from Paul: "Get off the backs of the Jews, and leave them in the hands of God."[59]

These examples indicate that Charles Cosgrove may be right in suggesting that a text like Rom 9–11, replete with unresolvable ambiguities, becomes a mirror for us to see and examine not Paul's views on the future of Israel but our own convictions about that future.

> Paul's text invites our interpretive wills to play a constitutive role in determining the meaning of Romans 11. . . . Hence we might expand the implicit hermeneutical directive of Romans 11 as follows:
>
>> To read me [that is, the text] rightly, you must deliberate with *me* about what *you* want the identity and destiny of carnal Israel to be. If you refuse to deliberate, you have not given me a fair hearing. If you accept, you become co-accountable for what my text means.[60]

Lodge draws a similar conclusion. This ambiguous text, he says, challenges the preconceived ideas of all readers regarding their present relationship to Israel and provokes all of them to come to a new understanding of that relationship.[61]

That may, indeed, be what Paul did.

Chapter Seven

"Then Comes the End . . ."

The Parousia and the Resurrection of the Dead

Paul's letters are liberally sprinkled with references to final events: Parousia, resurrection, judgment. These are usually brief statements, reminders of what the readers already know and mentioned to support a warning, an encouragement, or an exhortation.[1] In only a few passages does Paul describe these final events in any detail, and when he does the description is shaped by the rhetorical needs of his immediate argument.[2] What emerges from the letters, then, is not a clear doctrine, but a mosaic of descriptive elements that form an uneasy whole.

Hellenistic Judaism itself embraced a mosaic of different expectations. Some Jews were apocalyptic, expecting a cosmic resolution of contemporary distress and injustice. Others were not. Some Jews anticipated a resurrection. Others did not.[3] Those who did look forward to a resurrection of the dead did not agree on how that resurrection would take place. Part of the problem was the difference between Hebrew and Greek notions of the body. The view reflected in Hebrew scripture is that the body and the *nepeš* (often translated "soul" but meaning something like "personhood") form an indissoluble whole in life and that neither survive death. Some biblical texts refer to the "ghosts" or "spirits" of the dead, but these were consigned to Sheol, the dark and silent final destination for all.[4] A prevailing view in the Greco-Roman world, however, was that the soul (*psychē*) was an immortal entity, distinct from the mortal body and separated from it at death. Indeed, it was often viewed as trapped in the body, only to be released at death for its heavenly ascent.[5] As Jews came in contact with Greek culture to form Hellenistic (that is, Greek-influenced) Judaism, these two views combined in a variety of ways.

Most Hellenistic Jewish writings that speak of resurrection reflect a belief in the resurrection of the body, but not all.[6] *Jubilees* 23 and *1 Enoch* 102–104

87

refer to a resurrection of spirits, and Wisdom of Solomon 1–6 and 4 Maccabees appropriate Hellenistic language and thought even more fully and focus on the immortality of the soul.[7] The writings that refer to resurrection of the body presume a single, future eschatological event in which all the bodies of the dead[8] will be simultaneously raised to judgment. Belief in the resurrection of spirits or the immortality of souls allows more variation in the eschatological timetable of events. There can be a single eschatological judgment in which all participate (so, apparently, *1 Enoch* 22 and *Jubilees* 23), or the spirit/soul of each person can face judgment immediately upon death (so, apparently, *Testament of Asher* 6 and 4 Macc 14:5; 16:13; 18:23). The first option in particular raises the question of the intermediate state of these spirits or souls, yet the question is rarely directly addressed (see, however, *1 Enoch* 22). Most documents that posit a resurrection of spirits or souls do not seem to presume (or they explicitly deny) that bodies will also be raised; *4 Ezra*, however, speaks of a resurrection of the body in which it will be rejoined with the soul (7:32) and then transformed to shine like light (7:97).

There is also a recurring but not consistent motif that those who have died in religious persecution will receive special treatment. In Dan 12 the martyrs of Antiochus's persecution are the only ones whose bodies are resurrected to eternal life, while "those who bring many to righteousness" (probably the leaders who helped the righteous maintain their faith) receive special glory.[9] In 4 Maccabees (and perhaps also Wisdom 1–6 and *Jubilees* 23) immediate transition into heaven seems to be reserved for those who died in religious persecution.

Characteristic of most of these texts, though, is ambiguity. Like Paul, the authors usually did not spell out clear and consistent views. They spoke primarily in word pictures and metaphors. And, obviously, the writings do not all present the same view. "The evidence indicates that in the intertestamental period [i.e., 200 BCE–100 CE] there was no single Jewish orthodoxy on the time, mode, and place of resurrection, immortality, and eternal life."[10] Paul's comments on these matters, though sharpened by his belief in the resurrection and imminent return of Jesus Christ, also show some ambiguity and—perhaps—inconsistency or development.

Resurrection at the Parousia
(1 Thessalonians and 1 Corinthians)

In what is probably Paul's earliest surviving letter, 1 Thessalonians, he writes at length about the events that will attend the end. His treatment of these matters is, however, far from comprehensive, for he is addressing one particular question about the end, and he leaves other issues on the side. The question that has been raised is not clearly articulated. It concerns some members of the church who have died prior to the coming of the Lord and the grief of their surviving friends and relatives (4:13). This grief does not seem to have arisen because the survivors doubt the resurrection, for Paul's argument is based on their common faith that Jesus died and rose again (4:14). Rather, what seems to have caused the Thessalonian believers such grief is the concern that those who have died before Christ returns will miss out on the glorious events of his return.[11] Those who survive until the Parousia—and Paul includes himself among those likely to do so—will be caught up in a bodily assumption to welcome the Lord as he descends from heaven;[12] those who have died will be raised at the final resurrection of the dead. If the resurrection of the dead follows the assumption of the living, the dead in Christ will be excluded from the drama of the Parousia and the joy of meeting the Lord. *Fourth Ezra* reflects a similar concern: "Woe to those who will survive in those days! And still more, woe to those who do not survive! For those who do not survive will be sorrowful, because they understand what is in store for the last days, but not attaining it" (13:16–18).[13]

The whole thrust of Paul's response is to correct this perception that those who have died will be at a disadvantage during the unfolding of eschatological events. It would, of course, be only a temporary and relative disadvantage since the dead would ultimately be raised to eternal life. But the disadvantage was perceived to be serious enough that survivors were consumed with grief "as others do who have no hope" (1 Thess 4:13). Paul consoles and corrects them with a word of the Lord:

> For this we declare to you by the word of the Lord, that we who are alive, who are left until the coming of the Lord, will by no means precede those who have died. For the Lord himself, with a cry of command, with the archangel's call and with the sound of God's trumpet, will descend from heaven, and the dead in Christ will rise first. Then we who are alive, who are left, will be caught up in the clouds together with them to meet the Lord in the air; and so we will be with the Lord forever. (4:15–17)

Though both the origin of this "word of the Lord" and its extent are disputed,[14] the message that Paul sends through it is clear. The dead are at no disadvantage whatsoever. (The Greek words translated "will by no means precede" are very emphatic and probably correct the erroneous view that those who are alive will precede the dead.) In fact, says Paul, the first event that will transpire when the Lord comes will be the raising of the dead to life so that they can participate along with the survivors in the meeting with the Lord.[15]

The Parousia is described with traditional apocalyptic imagery, yet Paul's use of that imagery is remarkably restrained (cf. Mark 13; 2 Thess 1:7–10; and, of course, Revelation). He does not comment on the status of the dead before their resurrection, except to refer to them as "asleep" (1 Thess 4:13–15; 5:10; see NRSV textual notes). This was a common metaphor for death, so whether Paul meant to suggest that the dead existed in an unconscious state is disputed. It is possible, but not certain.[16] Paul does not mention the transformation of their bodies at the resurrection. He does not say what will happen when the newly resurrected and the still living meet the Lord or where they will be when they are with him forever.[17] His focus is on one single point: that all believers—the still living and the newly resurrected—will experience these events together. "The community of Christians crosses even the boundary of death."[18]

In Corinth a different issue had arisen concerning the end-time events. Some in the community were asserting that "there is no resurrection of the dead" (1 Cor 15:12). By this they seemed to deny not resurrection per se (see 15:11) but the resurrection of the dead *body*, basing their hopes instead on the immortality of the soul or spirit.[19] Another prevalent interpretation is that the Corinthians embraced a "realized eschatology": through their reception of the Spirit they had already entered a form of angelic existence that made the resurrection of the body irrelevant (see 4:8; 13:1). Denial of the resurrection of the dead was, according to this interpretation, a denial that the resurrection is still future.[20] Whatever the Corinthians' views, though, Paul responds by offering various arguments for the resurrection of the dead (15:12–34). Central to all of these is Christ's own resurrection from the dead, which, he says, they had come to believe (v. 11).

Because the Corinthian position was rooted in a view of the body as inherently mortal and corruptible and therefore incapable of resurrection, Paul devotes a large portion of his argument to the question of how dead bodies are raised (vv. 35–57). Using the metaphor of the seed, Paul explains that there will be a transformation. The physical, perishable, earthly body will be transformed into a suitable heavenly entity: a body that is spiritual, imperishable, clothed in glory, different in substance from its earthly counterpart but nevertheless continuous with it. Metaphors ultimately fell short of the reality that Paul was attempting to describe, and he spoke finally of a "mystery" that echoed his message to the Thessalonians: "Listen, I will tell you a mystery! We will not all die, but we will all be changed, in a moment, in the twinkling of an eye, at the last trumpet. For the trumpet will sound, and the dead will be raised imperishable, and we will be changed. For this perishable body must put on imperishability and this mortal body must put on immortality" (1 Cor 15:51–53). The same components are present here as in the Thessalonian letter. At the sound of the trumpet (the trumpet that in 1 Thessalonians heralds the Parousia) the dead will be raised and all will be changed, both those newly raised to life and those who remained alive. In 1 Thessalonians the emphasis was on a change of location—all will be snatched up together to meet the Lord. Here the emphasis is on a change in the nature of the body—the perishable body puts on imperishability.

As in 1 Thessalonians, the fate of nonbelievers is not in view. There is no reference here to judgment (cf. 1 Thess 5:3–9), though comments elsewhere in the letter indicate that the Parousia will include a judgment of all (1 Cor 1:8; 3:12–15). What is clear from these two passages is that Paul expected the Parousia to happen soon (in both letters Paul identifies himself with the "we" who will be alive to see it). He expected the resurrection of the dead to occur at the Parousia; and especially in 1 Corinthians he insists that it will be the body that is resurrected—a changed body, a "spiritual body," but definitely the body. He does not give much attention to the status of the dead before the resurrection, except to say in 1 Corinthians that the bodies of the dead are sown in the dust, where they await the instantaneous transformation ("in the twinkling of an eye") that will occur at the sound of the last trumpet. Are the spirits of the dead also quiescent in this interim? Paul does not directly say so in this letter, though once again he uses the language of "sleep" to describe the condition of the dead (15:20). In 2 Corinthians, however, he may reflect more fully on that question.

The Naked Soul?
(2 Cor 4:16–5:10)

This passage is notoriously difficult. Paul mixes metaphors and argues with frustrating imprecision. He uses Hellenistic categories of thought that introduce a new element of body-soul dualism into his reflections on death, but he uses them in such a way that it is not clear how fully he embraced such ideas. In this letter Paul is desperately seeking to discredit his opponents and their ideas, just as they have sought to discredit him. His words are often filled with irony, which immensely complicates the task of interpretation. When is he mocking his opponents' views, and when is he stating his own? Presumably the original recipients of the letter could tell (especially it were read with expression by Paul's envoy). We, however, often cannot. An additional problem is the Greek text itself, which at key points can be translated in a variety of ways. Interpretations of this passage are thus widely divergent, with good arguments for many but compelling arguments for none.

In the context of discussing the afflictions that attend his apostolic ministry (4:7–11), Paul assures his readers that "we do not lose heart" (4:16). Initially he describes the basis for this confidence in terms familiar from his earlier letters: "We know that the one who raised the Lord Jesus will raise us also with Jesus, and will bring us with you into his presence" (4:14). Here he speaks, as he did in 1 Cor 15 and 1 Thess 4, of a general resurrection of the faithful followed by an assumption into the divine presence. He continues, though, to reflect on his confidence by referring to an outer person that is wasting away and an inner person that is being renewed (4:16), an earthly tent that is being destroyed and an eternal heavenly dwelling that awaits habitation (5:1), a reference to being "found naked" (5:3), and a contrast between being unclothed and being further clothed (5:4). This way of speaking seems quite dualistic.

Some interpret this language as a reflection on the interim state of the soul of one who dies before the Parousia. Paul describes this state in terms of nakedness and (apparently) awareness: the soul has been stripped of the mortal body and awaits reclothing with a spiritual body at the Parousia.[21] Paul seems to contemplate this possibility of bodiless existence with some alarm—the very language of "nakedness," an anathema to Jews, suggests this: He longs instead to have the spiritual body put on over the earthly body—that is, to survive until the Parousia and to have his living body transformed at the sound of the last trumpet (1 Cor 15:52). This line of interpretation seems to fit well into Paul's emphasis on his present afflictions, extending them—at least rhetorically—into the interim state. If correct, Paul's basic conception of eschatological events (Parousia, resurrection, assumption) remains unchanged. What has changed is that Paul now envisions the possibility of dying before the Parousia and reflects more carefully on the interim state of the dead.[22]

Other verses in this passage, however, point to a different conception of the sequence of events. When Paul says, "For we know that if the earthly tent we live in is destroyed, *we have* a building from God, a house not made with hands, eternal in the heavens" (2 Cor 5:1), he seems to suggest that immediately upon death an individual will inhabit a heavenly dwelling (that is, receive a spiritual body) and be at home with the Lord (see also v. 8).[23] What, then, of the reference to nakedness? There are a couple of options. It could have been meant in a moral sense, a description of a state of guilt, of lacking a garment of "righteousness" in which to appear before God.[24] Similarly, it could allude to alienation from Christ. Having "put on" Christ at baptism, one could fall away, become "naked," and lose salvation (see Gal 3:28).[25] This line of argument suits the final exhortation of the passage well: "For all of us must appear before the judgment seat of Christ, so that each may receive recompense for what has been done in the body, whether good or evil" (5:10).

Alternatively, the dualistic language of the passage, including the language of nakedness, could be part of Paul's attack on the "false apostles" in Corinth (11:13). *They* emphasized a spirituality that reflected the glory of the risen Lord in their present existence. In response, *Paul* emphasized the contrast and temporal distance between the earthly tent that believers now inhabit and the heavenly dwelling that will be theirs, but only in the future. The Corinthians may have been so caught up in the spirituality of the false apostles that they no longer contemplated or anticipated a future resurrection body. Paul suggests that the logical outcome of that view was a state of nakedness of the soul and asserts in opposition "that the final state of the believer is not one of disembodiment: having received the 'spiritual body' [immediately upon death], he will never be found in a bodiless state."[26] This is an appealing reading that is well suited to the polemical tone of the letter, but it depends too heavily on conjectures about what others were saying to be secure.

Paul's language is too imprecise to allow a confident decision about his intended meaning. My own preference is for the first. It seems to allow the most straightforward reading of the text, but it still creates some difficulties. What is common to all the readings, however, is the emphasis on Paul's absolute confidence in the ultimate outcome. The final state is not the nakedness of a disembodied soul but a new spiritual body, and "He who has prepared us for this very thing is God, who has given us the Spirit as a guarantee" (5:5).

To Depart and Be [Immediately] with Christ (Phil 1:21–24)

Paul's comments to the Philippians on after-death existence are remarkably clear, and (perhaps) remarkably different from his earlier comments (depending on the interpretation of 2 Cor 5 that is adopted). At the time he wrote this letter, the apostle was in prison and facing the very real possibility of execution. In that situation he reflected with remarkable equanimity on the relative advantages of living and dying. Living means the fruitful labor of proclaiming the gospel, but dying means being with Christ: "I am hard pressed between the two: my desire is to depart and be with Christ, for that is far better; but to remain in the flesh is more necessary for you" (Phil 1:23–24). Paul's concern for his churches resolved the dilemma for him: "I know that I will remain and continue with all of you for your progress and joy in the faith" (v. 25). Yet the rejected, rather, the *postponed* alternative—to depart and be with Christ—indicates rather unambiguously that when writing this letter Paul expected to be with Christ, that is, in heaven, immediately upon his death. There is no reference here to an anxious interim period of nakedness, no reference to the Parousia as the occasion of resurrection, transformation, and assumption. Paul's views on the timing of the resurrection have clearly changed.

Yet the picture becomes murkier when we look at the rest of the letter. In chapter 3 Paul seems to revert to the Parousial expectations he expressed in 1 Corinthians and 1 Thessalonians: "But our citizenship is in heaven, and it is from there that we are expecting a Savior, the Lord Jesus Christ. He will transform our humble bodies that they may be conformed to his glorious body, by the power that also enables him to make all things subject to himself" (3:20–21, following the alternate readings of the NRSV textual notes). Here he speaks again of expecting (or "awaiting," NAB) the arrival from heaven of the Lord Jesus Christ. At that time, that is, at the Parousia, Christ will transform earthly bodies into bodies of heavenly glory and the displaced citizens of heaven (the faithful) will at last enter their true commonwealth.

How are these two views, expressed in the same letter, to be reconciled?[27] One can argue that 1:20 speaks of the soul's immediate departure to be with Christ, while 3:21 speaks of the parousial transformation of the body and (presumably) its reunion with the already heaven-dwelling soul (as in *4 Ezra* 7). Alternatively, 1:20 could speak of the life after death, now understood to be a life with Christ immediately upon death, while 3:21 speaks of the transformation of the living at the Parousia. Neither of these distinctions is clearly indicated in the text, but in either case this would mark a shift from Paul's earlier view that the dead were resurrected and united with Christ only at the Parousia.

There is, however, a third possibility. Only in Philippians 1 does Paul use the first person singular to speak of life after death. That is, only in this passage does he reflect on life after death exclusively in terms of his own future.[28] And only in this letter does he write about this from prison while awaiting possible execution. Did he regard immediate transition to the presence of Christ to be a special reward for a martyr's death?[29] If so, his view of the basic eschatological timetable could remain unchanged: most of the dead in Christ would be raised at the Parousia. Like the martyrs of old, though, after his execution he would receive an immediate reward for his faithfulness (see 4 Macc 9:8, 22; 13:17; 14:5; 17:12).

The Cosmos and the Parousia
(Rom 8:18–25)

Paul does not mention the Parousia in his letter to the Romans. He does, however, allude to the bodily transformation of the faithful that would attend it (8:18, 23; cf. Phil 3:21). There is no discussion of the nature of this transformation (as there is in 1 Corinthians), nor of the assumption of the transformed bodies into heaven (as there is in 1 Thessalonians), nor of the possibility of immediate transition to heaven at death (as there is in Philippians). There is, however, a new element: Paul here envisions the cosmic dimensions of the parousial transformation.

As in 2 Corinthians, Paul uses the metaphor of groaning in labor pains (Rom 8:22–23; cf. 2 Cor 5:2–4) to describe the current anguish and eager longing of the faithful for their transformation: "We ourselves, who have the first fruits of the Spirit, groan inwardly while we wait for adoption, the redemption of our bodies." Now, though, Paul asserts that all creation is groaning too, and that when the faithful receive their resurrection bodies, the whole creation will share in that transformation.[30] "Creation itself will be set free from its bondage to decay and will obtain the freedom of the glory of the children of God" (8:21).

This is a stunning and provocative shift. Apocalyptic scenarios often envisioned a new heaven and earth, but that was usually achieved only through the destruction of the old (see Mark 13:24–27; Rev 16; 21; Isa 24). In Galatians Paul himself spoke of redemption *from* the present evil age (1:4) and of being crucified to the world as the world was crucified to him (6:15). Here he emphasizes solidarity with the world instead, solidarity with both its present groaning and bondage and with its future redemption. The unbroken solidarity of the community of the faithful at the Parousia that he envisioned in 1 Thessalonians has here been expanded to include all of creation.

Conclusion

Paul's comments on the Parousia and the resurrection present a challenging mosaic of ideas. They can be interpreted to form a reasonably coherent picture, or they can be taken as evidence of a development (or flexibility) in Paul's views. Either way, Paul conceived end-time events within the parameters of first-century Jewish thought; yet he explored the implications of these events in light of his encounter with the resurrected Christ and in response to the needs and concerns of his churches. The result is a rich complexity that stimulates reflection.

Behind all the flexibility and complexity (and ambiguity) of Paul's comments on the future lies his fixed certitude about what God has already done in the past. God has raised Jesus from the dead—an event that signaled for Paul that the turn of the ages and the general resurrection was at hand (1 Cor 15:20). More than a mere sign of the end, though, the resurrection of Jesus was also a guarantee that God will raise those who have been united with Christ through baptism (Rom 6:5). God has also supplied the Spirit to the faithful as a down payment on and guarantee of the eschatological glory that is to be theirs (2 Cor 8:5). Here, then, lies the true basis for Christian hope. *That* God will remain faithful to the faithful is certain, even in death. *How* God will do it remains, as Paul acknowledged, a mystery.

Endnotes

Chapter 1: Grace

1. For surveys of the evolving debate, see, e.g., Stephen Westerholm, *Israel's Law and the Church's Faith: Paul and His Recent Interpreters* (Grand Rapids: Eerdmans, 1988); idem, *Perspectives Old and New on Paul: The "Lutheran" Paul and His Critics* (Grand Rapids: Eerdmans, 2004); Donald A. Hagner, "Paul and Judaism: The Jewish Matrix of Early Christianity: Issues in the Current Debate," *BBR* 3 (1993): 111–30.

2. There are, however, a number of scholars who would qualify that premise. Hendrikus Boers, e.g., challenges the statement that "in Paul, χάρις [grace] is the central concept which expresses most clearly his understanding of the event of salvation" (*TDNT* 9:393). That claim, Boers says, "is valid in the sense that that is what the term came to mean in Galatians and Romans but not what it meant in Paul's thinking in all his letters" ("Ἀγάπη and χάρις in Paul's Thought," *CBQ* 59.4 [1997]: 693–713, quotation on 705). And Francis Watson asserts that "the idea that salvation occurs *solely* through God's grace represents a deep misunderstanding of Paul" (*Paul, Judaism and the Gentiles* [SNTSMS 56; Cambridge: Cambridge University Press, 1986], 120, emphasis mine).

3. See Karl P. Donfried, "Justification and Last Judgment in Paul," *Int* 30.2 (1976): 140–52; Kent L. Yinger, *Paul, Judaism, and Judgment according to Deeds* (SNTSMS 105; Cambridge: Cambridge University Press, 1999).

4. E. P. Sanders, *Paul and Palestinian Judaism: A Comparison of Patterns of Religion* (Philadelphia: Fortress, 1977). See also his essay "Judaism and the Grand 'Christian' Abstractions: Love, Mercy, and Grace," *Int* 39.4 (1985): 357–72.

5. This primacy of grace in Judaism was recognized in James Moffatt's good but now dated study *Grace in the New Testament* (New York: Long & Smith, 1932); he nevertheless insisted dogmatically that "one of [Christianity's] *most distinctive truths* was the truth of grace" (392, emphasis mine).

6. 1QH 7:16–18; the translation is that of Geza Vermes, *The Dead Sea Scrolls in English* (4th ed.; Sheffield: Sheffield Academic Press, 1995).

7. Sanders himself admits as much: "On the point at which many have found the decisive contrast between Paul and Judaism—grace and works—Paul is in agreement with Palestinian Judaism. . . . *Salvation is by grace but judgment is according to works; works are the*

condition of remaining 'in,' but they do not earn salvation" (*Paul*, 543). Sanders sees the difference to lie elsewhere—in Paul's "participationist eschatology," that is, the conviction that "one participates in salvation by becoming one person with Christ" (549). See also Morna D. Hooker, "Paul and 'Covenantal Nomism,'" in *Paul and Paulinism: Essays in Honour of C. K. Barrett* (ed. M. D. Hooker and S. G. Wilson; London: SPCK, 1982), 47–56.

8. See also Hans Conzelmann and Walther Zimmerli, "χάρις, κτλ.," *TDNT* 9:372–91; Moffatt, *Grace*, 21–72.

9. As Boers notes, in none of this does Paul "move beyond anything expressed by that word [i.e., *charis*] in his Greek and Hebrew-Jewish background" ("Ἀγάπη," 705).

10. So Watson, *Paul*, 66.

11. Sanders, *Paul*, 157–82. The only exception is the sin of rejecting God and God's covenant, but even those who do that may repent and be restored to covenant grace (168). Paul's silence on this matter is notorious.

12. "In Judaism sin is uniformly transgression" (Sanders, *Paul*, 546). The rabbinic concept of the "evil inclination" seems close to Paul's thought, but the rabbis always assumed that a person had the power to resist this inclination (see Solomon Schechter, *Aspects of Rabbinic Theology* [1909; repr., New York: Schocken, 1961], 242–92).

13. So Westerholm, *Israel's Law*, 142; see also Timo Laato, *Paul and Judaism: An Anthropological Approach* (SFSHJ 115; Atlanta: Scholars Press, 1995), 75–77; Brad Eastman, *The Significance of Grace in the Letters of Paul* (New York: Peter Lang, 1999), 207–8; Douglas J. Moo, "'Law,' 'Works of the Law,' and Legalism in Paul," *WTJ* 45.1 (1983), 73–100, esp. 98.

14. Thus I disagree with Moffatt's conclusion that this is a distinctive feature of the Christian message of grace (*Grace*, 6), and with Boers's separation of this meaning from those he describes as "traditional usage" ("Ἀγάπη," 106–8).

15. For examples, see Sanders, *Paul*, esp. 105–6, 125–58, 168–72.

16. Not, of course, in all branches of the early church. Atonement Christology is muted in the Gospel of John, and absent altogether from the Q traditions and the *Gospel of Thomas*.

17. See, on this, Charles B. Cousar, *A Theology of the Cross: The Death of Jesus in the Pauline Letters* (OBT; Minneapolis: Fortress, 1990), esp. 52–87.

18. It is the Greek verb *charizomai*, not the noun *charis* ("grace"), that is present in this verse. The basic meaning of the verb is "to grant or to give freely," and one could argue that it does not necessarily carry the distinctive theological implications of grace (so, e.g., Boers, "Ἀγάπη," 699). However, since the verse echoes the earlier statement of 1:7, in which Paul notes that the Philippians share with him in God's grace as it is manifested both in his imprisonment and in his proclamation, it seems reasonable to claim the full force of the theological meaning for the verb. It is certainly taken that way by most commentators and by Moffatt (*Grace*, 165–66.).

19. See Cousar, *Cross*, 135–89.

20. Paul speaks in several passages of sharing in Christ's suffering, though without linking it, as he does here, with grace; see Rom 8:17; 2 Cor 1:5; 4:10–11; Gal 2:19; Phil 3:10–11. On the social implications of this, see Wayne A. Meeks, "The Social Context of Pauline Theology," *Int* 36.3 (1982): 266–77.

21. For a discussion of this peculiar Pauline construction (Greek *pisteuein eis Christon*, lit. "to believe into Christ"), see Sam K. Williams, "Again *Pistis Christou*," *CBQ* 49.3 (1987): 431–47.

22. It was not that followers of Christ were to seek out suffering in order to be conformed to Christ's death. Rather, their identification with a crucified Messiah gave them a new way of interpreting their experience; see Calvin J. Roetzel, "'As Dying, and Behold We Live': Death and Resurrection in Paul's Theology," *Int* 46.1 (1992): 5–18, esp. 9.

23. It is therefore particularly prominent in the letters to the Corinthians and to the Philippians.

24. See Millicent C. Feske, "Christ and Suffering in Moltmann's Thought," *Asbury Theological Journal* 55 (2000): 85–104.

25. Note the care with which Cousar discusses the topic of the suffering of the church (*Cross*, esp. 175).

26. Rudolf Bultmann, *Theology of the New Testament* (2 vols.; New York: Scribner's, 1951–55), 1:264.

27. Ibid., 243. Though Bultmann sees self-reliance as the *human* condition, he regards Judaism as its consummate expression.

28. See, e.g., Hans Hübner, *Law in Paul's Thought* (Edinburgh: T. & T. Clark, 1984),101–24; Robert H. Gundry, "Grace, Works, and Staying Saved in Paul," *Bib* 66.1 (1985): 1–38.

29. Heikki Räisänen provides the helpful label "soft legalism" for this sort, and "hard legalism" for that characterized by self-righteousness ("Legalism and Salvation by the Law," in *The Torah and Christ* [Helsinki: Finnish Exegetical Society, 1986], 25–54).

30. Westerholm, *Israel's Law*, 142; see also n. 12 above.

31. Ibid., 165.

32. The clearest support for this interpretation is found in Rom 3:20–24.

33. Westerholm, *Israel's Law*, 166–67.

34. This is the interpretation preferred by Sanders, *Paul*, 474–508; Räisänen, "Legalism," 27.

35. It finds strongest support in Gal 2:21; see J. Louis Martyn, *Galatians* (AB 33A; New York: Doubleday, 1997), 259–60.

36. Räisänen, e.g., notes that we know nothing about Jewish piety in the specific environs of Galatia. An errant, legalistic version of Judaism could have existed there, and Paul's mistake would have been his generalizations from this localized phenomenon ("Legalism," 41).

37. See, e.g., Francis Watson, *Paul, Judaism and the Gentiles: A Sociological Approach* (Cambridge: Cambridge University Press, 1986), passim; Räisänen ("Legalism," 46–53) presents a more innocent reconstruction of events.

38. See, e.g., Krister Stendahl, "The Apostle Paul and the Introspective Conscience of the West," *HTR* 56.3 (1963): 199–215; James D. G. Dunn, "The New Perspective on Paul: Paul and the Law," *Romans 1–8* (WBC 38A; Dallas: Word, 1988), lxiii–lxxii; John M. G. Barclay, "'Neither Jew nor Greek': Multiculturalism and the New Perspective on Paul," in *Ethnicity and the Bible* (ed. M. G. Brett; Biblical Interpretation Series 19; Leiden: Brill, 1996), 197–214.

39. Moffatt long ago suggested that there are two "foci" of Paul's view of grace: it excludes all merit and all racial distinctions (*Grace*, 9); more recently I. Howard Marshall has insisted that "we are not forced into the either/or of the newer and the more traditional understandings" ("Salvation, Grace and Works in the Later Writings in the Pauline Corpus," *NTS* 42.3 [1996]: 356–57).

40. Dunn, "New Perspective," lxxi.

41. Thus, specifically, Boers, "Ἀγάπη," 710.

42. See Marshall, "Salvation," 347; P. T. O'Brien, "Justification in Paul and Some Crucial

Issues of the Last Two Decades," in *Right with God: Justification in the Bible and the World* (ed. D. A. Carson; Grand Rapids: Baker, 1992), 68–95, esp. 69, 85.

43. Some find in Paul's letters a message of salvation for the Jews apart from Christ; see, e.g., Stanley K. Stowers, *A Rereading of Romans: Justice, Jews, and Gentiles* (New Haven: Yale University Press, 1994), 36–41; Lloyd Gaston, *Paul and the Torah* (Vancouver: University of British Columbia Press, 1987), 140–50. See chap. 6 below.

44. Barclay, "'Neither Jew nor Greek,'" 212–13; see also Watson, *Paul*, 180–81; S. G. Wilson, "Paul and Religion," in *Paul and Paulinism: Essays in Honour of C. K. Barrett* (ed. M. D. Hooker and S. G. Wilson; London: SPCK, 1982), 339–54.

45. Barclay, "'Neither Jew nor Greek,'" 213.

Chapter 2: Paul and the Jewish Law

1. *Nomos* can mean (among other things) "law" (in Paul's letters, either law in general or specifically the Mosaic law), "order," or "principle"; sometimes in Paul's letters it means "scripture" (as in Rom 3:19). See Michael Winger, *By What Law? The Meaning of* Νόμος *in the Letters of Paul* (SBLDS 128; Atlanta: Scholars Press, 1992).

2. See, e.g., Seyoon Kim, *Paul and the New Perspective: Second Thoughts on the Origin of Paul's Gospel* (Grand Rapids: Eerdmans, 2002), 1–84.

3. See, e.g., John W. Drane, *Paul: Libertine or Legalist?* (London: SPCK, 1975), 109–31.

4. See, e.g., William Wrede, *Paul* (London: Philip Green, 1907), 122–28; James D. G. Dunn, "The Incident at Antioch (Gal. 2.11–18)," in *Jesus, Paul, and the Law: Studies in Mark and Galatians* (Louisville: Westminster/John Knox, 1990), 129–74.

5. So Heikki Räisänen, *Paul and the Law* (WUNT 29; Philadelphia: Fortress, 1986), 199–202; E. P. Sanders, *Paul, the Law, and the Jewish People* (Philadelphia: Fortress, 1983), 143–54.

6. For a particularly intriguing analysis of this situation, see Paula Fredriksen, "Judaism, the Circumcision of Gentiles, and Apocalyptic Hope: Another Look at Galatians 1 and 2," *JTS*, n.s., 42.2 (1991): 532–64.

7. See Shaye J. D. Cohen, "Crossing the Boundary and Becoming a Jew," *HTR* 82.1 (1989): 13–33; Jerome H. Neyrey, "Bewitched in Galatia," *CBQ* 50.1 (1988): 72–100. Judith Lieu challenges this traditional view ("'Impregnable Ramparts and Walls of Iron': Boundary and Identity in Early 'Judaism' and 'Christianity,'" *NTS* 48.3 [2002]: 297–313).

8. See, e.g., Jonathan Z. Smith, "Fences and Neighbors: Some Contours of Early Judaism," in *Imagining Religion: From Babylon to Jonestown* (Chicago Studies in the History of Judaism; Chicago: University of Chicago Press, 1982), 1–18; John J. Collins, "A Symbol of Otherness: Circumcision and Salvation in the First Century," in *"To See Ourselves as Others See Us": Christians, Jews, "Others" in Late Antiquity* (ed. J. Neusner and E. S. Frerichs; Chico, CA: Scholars Press, 1985), 163–86. The issue is disputed; for opposing views see John Nolland, "Uncircumcised Proselytes?" *JSJ* 12.2 (1981): 173–94; Cohen, "Crossing the Boundary."

9. For a careful discussion of these Philonic passages, see Peder Borgen, *Paul Preaches Circumcision and Pleases Men and Other Essays on Christian Origins* (Trondheim: TAPIR, 1983); and idem, *Philo, John and Paul: New Perspectives on Judaism and Early Christianity* (Brown Judaic Studies 131; Atlanta: Scholars Press, 1987).

10. For an analysis of the probable circumstances reflected in this passage, see Smith, *Imagining Religion*, 12–13.

11. The translation is that of Lawrence H. Schiffman, *Who Was a Jew? Rabbinic and Halakhic*

Perspectives on the Jewish Christian Schism (Hoboken, NJ: Ktav, 1985), 33; for further discussion of this passage see Neil J. McEleney, "Conversion, Circumcision and the Law," *NTS* 20.3 (1974): 319–41.

12. The Hebrew equivalent is found in several documents from Qumran (4QFlor 1:7; 4QMMT 3:29; 1QS 5:21; 6:18).

13. This line of interpretation derives from Martin Luther, though it is now clear that Luther's legalistic interpretation of the Judaism of Paul's day was heavily influenced by his objections to the Catholicism of his own day. See Mark Reasoner, *Romans in Full Circle: A History of Interpretation* (Louisville: Westminster John Knox, 2005), 31–35.

14. The classic expression of this is found in Rudolf Bultmann, *Theology of the New Testament* (2 vols.; New York: Scribner's, 1951–55), 1:264; but see also Ernst Käsemann, *Romans* (Grand Rapids: Eerdmans, 1980), 89; and C. E. B. Cranfield, *Romans* (2 vols.; ICC; Edinburgh: T & T Clark, 1975–79), 1:164–65.

15. For example, Claude G. Montefiore, *Judaism and St. Paul: Two Essays* (London: Goschen, 1914), esp. 81–91; and more forcefully, Solomon Schechter, *Aspects of Rabbinic Theology* (1909; repr., New York: Schocken, 1961), 18; George F. Moore, *Judaism in the First Centuries of the Christian Era* (3 vols.; Cambridge: Harvard University Press, 1927–30), 2:282.

16. E. P. Sanders, *Paul and Palestinian Judaism: A Comparison of Patterns of Religion* (Philadelphia: Fortress, 1977).

17. Ibid., 17.

18. *Fourth Ezra*, which reflects only God's grace of election and not God's mercy of forgiveness, was the single exception; ibid., 409–18.

19. This is the general tone of the essays in D. A. Carson et al., eds., *Justification and Variegated Nomism*, vol. 1, *The Complexities of Second Temple Judaism* (Grand Rapids: Baker, 2001).

20. See, e.g., Francis Watson, *Paul, Judaism and the Gentiles: A Sociological Approach* (SNTSMS 56; Cambridge: Cambridge University Press, 1986), 34–38; Heikki Räisänen, "Legalism and Salvation by the Law," in *The Torah and Christ* (Helsinki: Finnish Exegetical Society, 1986), 25–54.

21. Sanders, *Paul and Palestinian Judaism*, 552.

22. See James D. G. Dunn, "The New Perspective on Paul," *BJRL* 65.1 (1983): 95–122; repr. in *Jesus, Paul, and the Law: Studies in Mark and Galatians* (Louisville: Westminster/John Knox, 1990), 183–206; see also idem, *Romans 1–8* (WBC 38A; Dallas: Word, 1988), lxiii–lxxii.

23. Charles H. Talbert's claim (complaint, really) that this revisionist view "has become critical orthodoxy" probably overstates the case ("Paul, Judaism, and the Revisionists," *CBQ* 63.1 [2001]: 1–22, esp. 13), though it has been embraced by a number of scholars; see, e.g., N. T. Wright, *The Climax of the Covenant: Christ and the Law in Pauline Theology* (Minneapolis: Fortress, 1992), 139 n. 10; Daniel Boyarin, *A Radical Jew: Paul and the Politics of Identity* (Berkeley: University of California Press, 1994), 51–52; William S. Campbell, *Paul's Gospel in an Intercultural Context: Jew and Gentile in the Letter to the Romans* (Studies in the Intercultural History of Christianity 69; Frankfort am Main: Lang, 1991), 127. For a glimpse of the ongoing, energetic debate, see the essays in James D. G. Dunn, ed., *Paul and the Mosaic Law* (Grand Rapids: Eerdmans, 2001); and in D. A Carson et al., eds., *Justification and Variegated Nomism*, vol. 2, *The Paradoxes of Paul* (Grand Rapids: Baker, 2004).

24. Tatha Wiley, *Paul and the Gentile Women: Reframing Galatians* (New York: Continuum, 2005), 78–102.

25. So Kim, *Paul and the New Perspective*, 61; see also Talbert, "Paul, Judaism, and the Revisionists," 14; Stanley K. Stowers, *A Rereading of Romans: Justice, Jews, and Gentiles* (New Haven: Yale University Press, 1994), 27–29; John G. Gager, *Reinventing Paul* (Oxford: Oxford University Press, 2000), 49.
26. For example, Kim, *Paul and the New Perspective*, 60; Simon J. Gathercole, *Where Is Boasting? Early Jewish Soteriology and Paul's Response in Romans 1–5* (Grand Rapids: Eerdmans, 2002), 266.
27. See Talbert, "Paul, Judaism, and the Revisionists," esp. 10; see also Carson et al., eds., *Justification and Variegated Nomism*, 1:543–48.
28. Talbert, "Paul, Judaism, and the Revisionists," 4.
29. Stephen Westerholm, *Israel's Law and the Church's Faith: Paul and His Recent Interpreters* (Grand Rapids: Eerdmans, 1988), 130–35; idem, *Perspectives Old and New on Paul: The "Lutheran" Paul and His Critics* (Grand Rapids: Eerdmans, 2004), 330–35; see also Räisänen, "Legalism," 26.
30. Westerholm, *Israel's Law*, 144; Talbert agrees that Paul had a "pessimistic anthropology," while Palestinian Judaism was more optimistic in its assessment of human ability ("Paul, Judaism, and the Revisionists," 16); see also Frank Thielman, *Paul and the Law: A Contextual Approach* (Downers Grove, IL: InterVarsity, 1994), 238–45.
31. So Stowers, *Rereading of Romans*, 187–88; Lloyd Gaston, *Paul and the Torah* (Vancouver: University of British Columbia Press, 1987), 140–50; Gager, *Reinventing Paul*, 59–61.
32. See Thielman's response to Gaston's and Gager's proposals in *From Plight to Solution: A Jewish Framework for Understanding Paul's View of the law in Galatians and Romans* (NovTSup 61; Leiden: Brill, 1989), 123–32.
33. Sanders, *Paul and Palestinian Judaism*, 442–47; many, but not all, agree with this presupposition. For an opposing view see Thielman, *From Plight to Solution*.
34. There seems to be a movement from both sides of the debate toward a middle ground that recognizes the presence of both elements in Paul's thought. Differences remain, however, on which element is central. See Gathercole, *Where Is Boasting?* 263–66; James D. G. Dunn, "In Search of Common Ground," in *Paul and the Mosaic Law*, ed. Dunn, 309–34; Thielman, *Paul and the Law*, 244.
35. So Leander E. Keck, *Romans* (ANTC; Nashville: Abingdon, 2005), 32–34; see also Dunn, "Common Ground," 325–34.
36. See J. Louis Martyn, "Apocalyptic Antinomies in Paul's Letter to the Galatians," *NTS* 31.3 (1985), 410–24.
37. Some have argued, however, that the reference is to evil angels or demonic beings; see Hübner, *Law in Paul's Thought*, 27–28.
38. This comment is notoriously difficult; see commentaries for discussions of interpretive options.
39. The "curse of the law" (v. 13) refers to the curse pronounced by the law on transgressions, not to the law as itself a curse; see James D. G. Dunn, *The Theology of Paul the Apostle* (Grand Rapids: Eerdmans, 1998), 225–27.
40. See Calvin J. Roetzel, *Paul: A Jew on the Margins* (Louisville: Westminster John Knox, 2003), 84.
41. The Greek is as ambiguous as the English. The race imagery in Rom 9:30–32 seems to provide strong support for the interpretation embraced here, but not all are convinced. For discussion see Robert Badenas, *Christ the End of the Law: Romans 10.4 in Pauline Perspective* (JSNTSup 10; Sheffield: JSOT Press, 1985).

42. See Gal 5:14 and 6:2.
43. Paul describes this Spirit as both the Spirit of God and the Spirit of Christ (v. 9). It is the sign that the recipient is currently a child of God (v. 16) and belongs to Christ (v. 9), and it serves as the "first fruits" of the salvation to come (v. 23).
44. For a survey of other interpretive options, most of which involve interpreting *nomos* as something like a principle or order (e.g., the principle of faith), see Dunn, *Theology*, 633; for a defense of the interpretation adopted here, see ibid., 634–58.
45. See Morna D. Hooker, "Paul and 'Covenantal Nomism,'" in *From Adam to Christ*, 155–64.
46. See, however, Fredriksen, "Judaism," 548–58.

Chapter 3: Faith

1. Today we would call them "Christians," but that title was not widely used until the 2nd century. It is not found in any of Paul's letters and appears in only three places in the entire NT (Acts 11:26; 26:28; 1 Pet 4:16).
2. A rough word count gives some indication of the significance of this concept for Paul. The noun *pistis* appears 8 times in Matthew, 5 times in Mark, 11 times in Luke, 15 times in Acts, and not at all in John. It appears 40 times in Romans alone and 51 times in the remaining undisputed Pauline letters, most prominently (after Romans) in Galatians (23 times). The disputed Pauline letters contain a total of 52 additional references to *pistis*. The word is also prominent in Hebrews (32 times), but primarily in chap. 11 (24 times), and in James (16 times), but primarily in chap. 2 (13 times). Overall, the Pauline corpus (both undisputed and disputed letters), which occupies about 22 percent of the New Testament, contains 59 percent of the references to *pistis*.
3. So Dieter Lührmann, "Faith: New Testament," *ABD* 2:751–52. David Hay is more cautious in his evaluation of the evidence: "Philo does not seem to give [*pistis* and *pisteuein*] anything like the central importance that they gain in Paul" ("*Pistis* as 'Ground for Faith' in Hellenized Judaism and Paul," *JBL* 108.3 [1989]: 461–76, esp. 464 n. 11).
4. See, e.g., *American Heritage Dictionary*, ad loc.
5. Less frequently Paul uses the word *pistis* to suggest the ground or basis for the human response (so Hay, "*Pistis*").
6. Luke T. Johnson, e.g., agrees with Rudolf Bultmann (*Theology of the New Testament* [2 vols.; New York: Scribner's, 1951–55], 1:314] that faith is primarily obedience ("Rom 3:21–26 and the Faith of Jesus," *CBQ* 44.1 [1982]: 85 n. 28); Lührmann insists that Paul's primary emphasis is on acceptance of the gospel, and thus on faith's content (*ABD* 2:753–54); and Richard B. Hays argues that Paul "is thinking primarily of the trust toward God that was prefigured by Abraham" ("ΠΙΣΤΙΣ and Pauline Christology: What Is At Stake?" in *Pauline Theology*, vol. 4, *Looking Back, Pressing On* [ed. E. E. Johnson and D. M. Hay; SBLSymS 4; Atlanta: Scholars Press, 1997], 35–60, esp. 59).
7. This is Philo's allegorical interpretation of the promise of land in Gen 15.
8. More fully titled the Wisdom of Jesus Son of Sirach, and also known as Ecclesiasticus.
9. NRSV; aspects of this translation will come under review later in the essay.
10. C. E. B. Cranfield, *Romans: A Shorter Commentary* (Grand Rapids: Eerdmans, 1985), 78.
11. Bultmann, *Theology*, 1:264.
12. Ibid., 1:315.
13. Ibid., 1:316.
14. Ibid., 1:314.

15. Ibid., 1:316.
16. Cranfield, *Shorter Romans*, 19.
17. As argued by E. P. Sanders, *Paul and Palestinian Judaism* (Philadelphia: Fortress, 1977).
18. James D. G. Dunn, *Romans 1–8* (WBC 38A; Dallas: Word, 1988), lxxii.
19. Ibid., 191, emphasis added.
20. Ibid., 192.
21. See chap. 2.
22. Most frequently no object is mentioned.
23. There is wide agreement on this point. See, e.g., Johnson, "Rom 3:21–26," 83–85; Hays, "ΠΙΣΤΙΣ," 53; Sam K. Williams, "Again *Pistis Christou*," *CBQ* 49.3 (1987): 43–47, esp. 434–35.
24. Abraham's trust is presented as a model for all believers; see Rom 4:11–12.
25. For example, Gal 2:16; Phil 1:29; Rom 9:3; 10:11. Johnson refers to this as "specifying confession," that is, it "not only sets Christians apart from pagans 'who do not know God' (1 Thess 4:5), but also from Jews, who have faith in the one God (Rom 2:17; 10:2), but who do not confess Jesus as Christ and Lord" ("Rom 3:21–26," 82).
26. Emphasized by Williams, who notes how striking it is that though Paul emphasizes that Christ is Lord, he does not (with a single ambiguous exception) speak of obedience to Christ ("Again *Pistis Christou*," 434–35 nn. 15, 16).
27. This support appears primarily in scholarly essays and monographs; the NRSV alone of recent translations acknowledges the "faith of Christ" alternative, but only in its textual notes.
28. "Subject" here is used grammatically, as in the "subject" of a verb. These genitives are associated only with nouns that indicate an action.
29. A more complete presentation of the arguments for and against each position, as well as generous footnotes listing supporters of the different readings, is provided by Hays, "ΠΙΣΤΙΣ," 35–60; James D. G. Dunn, "Once More, ΠΙΣΤΙΣ ΧΡΙΣΤΟΥ," in *Pauline Theology*, vol. 4, ed. Johnson and Hay, 61–81; and Paul J. Achtemeier, "Apropos the Faith of/in Christ," in *Pauline Theology*, vol. 4, 82–92.
30. See Mark Reasoner, *Romans in Full Circle: A History of Interpretation* (Louisville: Westminster John Knox, 2005), 23–41.
31. George Howard claims that these early translations strongly support the "faith of Christ" reading ("On the 'Faith of Christ'," *HTR* 60.4 [1967]: 459–84; idem, "Faith of Christ," *ABD* 2.758–60); Morna D. Hooker cautions that the Latin, at least, is as ambiguous as the Greek ("Πίστις Χριστοῦ," in *From Adam to Christ: Essays on Paul* [Cambridge: Cambridge University Press, 1990], 165–86, esp. 165–66).
32. The Greek text of Gal 3:26 also seems to contain this construction (*pistis* + *en* + Christ Jesus), but closer analysis has led to the general consensus that in this sentence "in Christ Jesus" is not the object of "faith." The NRSV translates it correctly as "in Christ Jesus you are all children of God through faith."
33. See Dunn, "Once More," 66–67.
34. "Christ's 'obedience' interprets his 'faithfulness'" (Leander E. Keck, "'Jesus' in Romans," *JBL* 108.3 [1989]: 443–60, quotation from 457; see also Richard B. Hays, *The Faith of Jesus Christ* [SBLDS 56; Chico, CA: Scholars Press, 1983], 175).
35. Howard reports one single example of the objective genitive in these writings (*ABD* 2:758–59).
36. So Michael Winger, "Act One: Paul Arrives in Galatia," *NTS* 48.4 (2002): 548–67, esp. 562; Keck, "'Jesus' in Romans," 453.

37. English translations consistently translate these phrases as "faith of . . ." It is only when the genitive noun is "Christ" (or a reference to Christ) that they use a "faith in . . ." translation.
38. *Faith of Jesus Christ*, 162.
39. See Howard, *ABD* 2:758.
40. In addition to reading the genitive as subjective rather than objective, this translation also eliminates the reference to *doing* works of the law, which is found in the NRSV but not in the original Greek text.
41. See Dunn, "Once More," 79.
42. Points (a) and (b) are noted by Hooker, "Πίστις Χριστοῦ," 166–67.
43. See Dunn, "Once More," 72, 80.
44. Hays, "ΠΙΣΤΙΣ," 56.
45. So Keck, "'Jesus' in Romans," 454 n. 39; Hays, "ΠΙΣΤΙΣ," 56.
46. So Keck, "'Jesus' in Romans," 454; but see Achtemeier, "Apropos," 88.
47. "Again *Pistis Christou*," 446.
48. Ibid., 445–46.
49. Ibid., 441.
50. Ibid., 439.
51. Ibid., 442.
52. Erwin R. Goodenough and A. T. Kraabel, "Paul and the Hellenization of Christianity," in *Religions in Antiquity: Essays in Memory of Erwin R. Goodenough* (ed. J. Neusner; Leiden: Brill, 1968), 23–68, esp. 45.
53. See Hooker, "Πίστις Χριστοῦ," 182–85; Hays, *Faith of Jesus Christ*, 260; idem, "ΠΙΣΤΙΣ," 52, 60.
54. Hooker, "Πίστις Χριστοῦ," 181.
55. Ibid. Hooker rejects this argument in favor of the notion of interchange. What follows here tracks the logic of transformative union instead.
56. Paul uses a different preposition (Greek *epi*, "on") to refer to believing or trusting or relying upon God (Rom 4:8, 24; see also Gal 3:6). In Rom 9:33 and 10:11 the preposition *epi* occurs in quotations from the Septuagint (originally referring to God), which Paul applies to Christ.
57. That is, they describe "the transfer to being in the group . . . who will be saved" (Sanders, *Paul*, 463).
58. Williams, "Again *Pistis Christou*," 443, emphasis original. For Williams, however, the important idea is believing like Christ, not moving into union with Christ; see the critique by Hays, "ΠΙΣΤΙΣ," 50–52.
59. Hooker, "Πίστις Χριστοῦ," 185–86.
60. As Dunn admits (and he favors the traditional interpretation), "For anyone who wishes to take the humanness of Jesus with full seriousness, 'the faith of Jesus' strikes a strong and resonant chord" ("Once More," 79).
61. See Hays, "ΠΙΣΤΙΣ," 56–57; George Howard, "On the 'Faith of Christ,'" HTR 60.4 (1967): 459–65, esp. 63–65.

Chapter 4: In Christ

1. Albert Schweitzer, *The Mysticism of Paul the Apostle* (New York: Henry Holt, 1931; original German edition, 1929), 22.
2. Rudolf Bultmann, *Theology of the New Testament* (2 vols.; New York: Scribner's, 1951–55), 1:335.
3. Schweitzer posed the alternatives in this way (*Mysticism*, 15).

4. Adolf Deissmann, *Paul: A Study in Social and Religious History* (2nd ed.; New York: Doran, 1926; original German edition, 1911), 187. The chronology of the important early-20th-century work on this topic is complex. Deissmann's was the first to appear in print, preceding Schweitzer's by 18 years; but the first draft of Schweitzer's book was, according to the preface, completed in 1909, two years before Deissmann's. Schweitzer's final draft was influenced by Deissmann's work as well as by the work of Wilhelm Bousset (*Kyrios Christos* [Göttingen: Vandenhoeck & Ruprecht, 1913]) and Richard Reitzenstein (*Die hellenistischen Mysterienreligionen* [Leipzig: Teubner, 1910]), both of whom had explored Paul's mysticism in the intervening years.

5. Deissmann, *Paul*, 166.

6. Bultmann defines the "Hellenistic Church" as the branch of the church that came under the influence of Gentile religions, especially mystery religions and Gnosticism (*Theology*, 1:63). Under this influence, he claims, the understanding of baptism as participation in Christ developed (1:140).

7. Bultmann, *Theology*, 1.311, emphasis his. Bultmann was not the first to reject a mystical element in Paul's writings. Since the end of the 19th century, German Protestant theology had been predominantly opposed to mysticism's role in Christianity and thus was reluctant to acknowledge it in Paul. Catholic theological and biblical scholars, on the other hand, tended to evaluate mysticism in general and Paul's mysticism in particular more positively. See the survey by Bernard McGinn, *The Foundations of Mysticism* (New York: Crossroad, 1991), 265–91; also William B. Barcley, *"Christ in You": A Study in Paul's Theology and Ethics* (Lanham, MD: University Press of America, 1999), 5–19.

8. Hans Conzelmann, *An Outline of the Theology of the New Testament* (New Testament Library; Philadelphia: Westminster, 1969; based on the 2nd German edition, 1968), 208–12, esp. 211.

9. Günther Bornkamm, *Paul* (New York: Harper & Row, 1971; original German edition, 1969), 155.

10. J. Christiaan Beker, *Paul the Apostle: The Triumph of God in Life and Thought* (Philadelphia: Fortress, 1980), 8.

11. Jürgen Becker, *Paul: Apostle to the Gentiles* (Louisville: Westminster/John Knox, 1993), 418.

12. For a cogent analysis of the factors behind this rejection, see James D. G. Dunn, *The Theology of Paul the Apostle* (Grand Rapids: Eerdmans, 1998), 391–95.

13. Michel Bouttier, *En Christ: Étude d'exégèse et de théologie pauliniennes* (Paris: Presses Universitaires de France, 1962).

14. Denys E. H. Whiteley, *The Theology of St. Paul* (Oxford: Blackwell, 1964), 130.

15. Ibid., 169.

16. Ernst Käsemann, "The Theological Problem Presented by the Motif of the Body of Christ," in *Perspectives on Paul* (Philadelphia: Fortress, 1969) 102–21, esp. 104 n. 9.

17. Ibid., 104.

18. E. P. Sanders, *Paul and Palestinian Judaism* (Philadelphia: Fortress, 1977), 459.

19. Ibid., 434; see also 434–72.

20. See, e.g., ibid., 435 n. 19; Schweitzer, *Mysticism*, 17; and p. 43 below.

21. Sanders, *Paul and Palestinian Judaism*, 522. The difficulty is reflected in the attempts to find explanatory options for Paul's "mystical" phrases. "Identify ourselves with him," "join up with him," "share together with him," "become close companions with him," "become just as though we were one person with him" are some alternatives that have

been proposed, but, as G. M. M. Pelser notes, these phrases do not reflect the same reality. That is, "becoming close companions" is not the same as "identifying oneself with," and neither expresses the same reality conveyed by "becoming one with him." See G. M. M. Pelser, "Could the 'Formulas' *Dying* and *Rising with Christ* Be Expressions of Pauline Mysticism?" *Neot* 32.1 (1998): 115–34, esp. 128; see also idem, "Once More the Body of Christ in Paul," *Neot* 32.2 (1998): 525–45, esp. 543.

22. John Ashton, *The Religion of Paul the Apostle* (New Haven: Yale University Press, 2000), 150–51.
23. In addition to the works cited, see also Morna D. Hooker, *From Adam to Christ: Essays on Paul* (Cambridge: Cambridge University Press, 1990), esp. section 1, "Interchange in Christ"; Richard N. Longenecker, *Galatians* (WBC 41; Dallas: Word, 1990); Calvin J. Roetzel, *Paul: The Man and the Myth* (Columbia, SC: University of South Carolina Press, 1998), 100–134; John Dominic Crossan and Jonathan L. Reed, *In Search of Paul* (San Francisco: HarperCollins, 2004), 277–84.
24. Scholars identify other "complementary" phrases that contribute to the notion of participation: "with Christ," "of Christ," "belonging to Christ"; see esp. Sanders, *Paul and Palestinian Judaism*, 453–63; Dunn, *Theology*, 390–412.
25. See, e.g., Rom 8:1–17; Gal 3:25–29; 2 Cor 5:11–21.
26. Elsewhere also in Phil 1:19 and Gal 4:6.
27. "Spirit" is capitalized, and thus identified as the Holy Spirit, in the Amplified Bible (1958), New Living Translation (1996), and Peterson (The Message; 1993).
28. Dunn, *Theology*, 264; italics original.
29. Definitions are important here. McGinn, seeking the broadest possible definition for his study of the history of Western Christian mysticism, equates mysticism with "the consciousness of . . . the immediate or direct presence of God" (McGinn, *Foundations of Mysticism*, xvii). When NT scholars refer to Paul's mysticism, however, they usually mean a sense of *union* with Christ that the language of "presence" does not adequately convey.
30. McGinn claims that "Paul does not seem to intend [the comment about becoming one spirit with the Lord] in any mystical sense" (*Foundations of Mysticism*, 74); but Sanders's very different assessment seems more attuned to Paul's logic (*Paul and Palestinian Judaism*, 454–55).
31. Dale B. Martin, *The Corinthian Body* (New Haven: Yale University Press, 1995), 186, 191.
32. Schweitzer regarded "in Christ" and "members of the [mystical] body of Christ" to be equivalent phrases (*Mysticism*, 122–23); again, Sanders agrees (*Paul and Palestinian Judaism*, 439). See also Käsemann, "Theological Problem," 106.
33. According to Dunn, the phrase "in Christ" or "in the Lord" appears 122 times in the undisputed Pauline letters (including Colossians). This number does not include the many instances in which a pronoun is used ("in him") (*Theology*, 396–97).
34. See Deismann, *Paul*, 140; Dunn, *Theology*, 399. The point is sometimes disputed (Schweitzer, *Mysticism*, 122–23; Sanders, *Paul and Palestinian Judaism*, 459 n. 35; Barcley, "*Christ in You*," 111–14), though given the fluidity of Paul's language, debates about what constitutes the central element of his mysticism are probably fruitless.
35. Dunn, *Theology*, 400.
36. Pelser, "Once More," 543.
37. Stoic influence is claimed for Paul's statements about the different members of the body working together in their different functions (1 Cor 12:14–31; Rom 12:3–8), but these passages clearly constitute a different category from the one under consideration here.

38. For a fuller version see Bultmann, *Theology*, 1:164–83.
39. John A. T. Robinson, *The Body: A Study in Pauline Theology* (SBT 1.5; London: SCM, 1952), 60.
40. See the assessments by Pelser, "Once More," 532–34; idem, "Formulas," 121–24; and Dunn, *Theology*, 548–52.
41. The longer phrase (with either the preposition "into" [Greek *eis*] or "in" [Greek *en*]) is found in Matt 26:19 (into), Acts 2:38 (in); 8:16 (into); 10:48 (in); and 19:5 (into).
42. So, e.g., George R. Beasley-Murray, *Baptism in the New Testament* (Grand Rapids: Eerdmans, 1962), 128–29.
43. So, e.g., Pelser, who asserts, "What is at issue here is a special and personal communion with Christ, which is of a different order to that of the believer as a member of the body of Christ in an ecclesiological sense" ("Once More," 540).
44. So Pelser, "Formulas," 124; Hans Dieter Betz, "Transferring a Ritual: Paul's Interpretation of Baptism in Romans 6," in *Paul in His Hellenistic Context* (ed. T. Engberg-Pedersen; Edinburgh: T & T Clark, 1994), 84–118, esp. 108. For nonmystical interpretations see Dunn, "'Baptized' as Metaphor," in *Baptism, the New Testament and the Church: Historical and Contemporary Studies in Honour of R. E. O. White* (ed. S. E. Porter and A. R. Cross; JSNTSup 171; Sheffield: Sheffield Academic Press, 1999), 298–99; idem, *Theology*, 453–54.
45. See, e.g., Pelser, "Formulas," 125; Sam K. Williams, "Again *Pistis Christou*," *CBQ* 49.3 (1987): 431–47, esp. 443.
46. Similar phrases, though using different language, are found in 2 Cor 4:10–11; 5:14–15; Gal 6:14, 17; Phil 3:10–11. Alastair Campbell notes that the words, "I have been crucified with Christ," are "a strikingly original phrase, a brutal wrenching of normal language, liable in a society that witnessed crucifixions at first hand to send shock waves through the audience" ("Dying with Christ: The Origin of a Metaphor?" in *Baptism, the New Testament and the Church*, ed. Porter and Cross, 273–93, esp. 282).
47. So Campbell, "Dying with Christ"; Robert Tannehill also rejects a mystical interpretation of the phrase, but avoids as well the conclusion that Paul speaks merely of imitation of Christ's suffering (*Dying and Rising with Christ: A Study in Pauline Theology* [BZNW 32; Berlin: Töpelmann, 1966]), 70.
48. So Pelser, "Formulas," 124–32.
49. It is also noteworthy that the passage continues with more assertions that suggest participation in Christ; see vv. 17, 21.
50. The Isis (Osiris) cult is the most frequently cited example, primarily because there are more written accounts of it. For a more complete discussion of the cult, see Reginald E. Witt, *Isis in the Ancient World* (Baltimore: Johns Hopkins University Press, 1971).
51. Campbell states that the idea that Paul's view of baptism derived from the mystery religions "has been exhaustively examined, and decisively rejected" ("Dying with Christ," 272).
52. Pelser, "Formulas," 121.
53. Dunn, "Metaphor," 306; Pelser, "Formulas," 122–23. Pelser's denial that a mystical union took place depends, in part, on his definition of "mystical" (see below). Like Pelser, Betz finds "many analogies" in Paul to the rites of the mystery religions ("Transferring a Ritual," 118).
54. Brook W. R. Pearson, "Baptism and Initiation in the Cult of Isis and Sarapis," in *Baptism, the New Testament and the Church*, ed. Porter and Cross, 42–62, esp. 48.

55. Dunn, "Metaphor," 306–7.
56. Dunn ("Metaphor") and Pelser ("Once More") provide helpful reminders that metaphor is a way of discussing a reality that cannot be expressed otherwise and should not be presented as reality's antithesis. Here, though, I refer to the use of "metaphor" as the opposite of "reality," a dichotomy that was applied to this topic at least as early as Schweitzer (*Mysticism*, 15).
57. Pelser, "Formulas," 132; Dunn agrees: "It [is] hard to avoid talk of something like a mystical sense of the divine presence of Christ within and without, establishing and sustaining the individual in relation to God" (*Theology*, 401).
58. Paul often emphasized that resurrection for the believer is a future event—his important "eschatological reservation" (e.g., 1 Cor 15:21–23; Rom 6:5). Yet there is a "newness of life" that the believer experiences in this life (Rom 6:4), and, though it is not full resurrection life, it does seem to be a strong foretaste of it ("a new creation," 2 Cor 5:17). Already in this life believers experience the power, though not the fullness, of Christ's resurrection (Phil 3:10).
59. Schweitzer, *Mysticism*, 15.
60. Schweitzer described this line of thought as a "subsidiary crater, which has formed within the rim of the main crater—the mystical doctrine of redemption through the being-in-Christ" (*Mysticism*, 225). Others explicitly or implicitly reverse the hierarchy.
61. Martin, *Corinthian Body*, 176.
62. Ibid., 131, quoting D. R. MacDonald; see also Halvor Moxnes, "Social Integration and the Problem of Gender in St. Paul's Letters," *Studia theologica* 43 (1989): 99–113; Lone Fatum, "Image of God and Glory of Man: Women in the Pauline Congregations," in *Image of God and Gender Models in Judaeo-Christian Tradition* (ed. K. E. Børresen; Oslo: Solum, 1991), 56–137; John S. Kloppenborg, "Egalitarianism in the Myth and Rhetoric of Pauline Churches," in *Reimagining Christian Origins: A Colloquium Honoring Burton L. Mack* (ed. E. A. Castelli and H. Taussig; Valley Forge, PA: Trinity Press International, 1996), 247–63.
63. For a more comprehensive exploration of this question, see Jouette M. Bassler, "The Problem of Self-Definition: What 'Self' and Whose Definition?" in *Redefining First-Century Jewish and Christian Identities: Essays in Honor of Ed. P. Sanders*, ed. F. E. Udoh (Notre Dame, IN: University of Notre Dame Press, forthcoming 2006).
64. *Gospel of Thomas* logion 114 is the most famous piece of evidence for this: "Simon Peter said to them: Let Mariham [Mary] go out from among us, for women are not worthy of the life. Jesus said: Look, I will lead her that I may make her male, in order that she too may become a living spirit resembling you males. For every woman who makes herself male will enter into the kingdom of heaven" (see *New Testament Apocrypha* [2 vols.; ed. W. Schneemelcher and R. McL. Wilson; rev. ed.; Louisville: Westminster John Knox, 1991–92], 1:120). The *Acts of Paul and Thecla* and the diary of Vibia Perpetua point in the same direction.
65. Gal 1:16; the NRSV translates this as "revealed his Son *to* me," but the Greek is unambiguously "*in* me," as the NRSV textual note correctly indicates. Other English translations present the phrase correctly (e.g., REB, NJB, KJV, NASB, NIV, Amplified Bible). Paul's own description of his conversion must be preferred to the accounts in Acts, which report this encounter as an external phenomenon (Acts 9:3; 22:6; 26:13).
66. Dunn, *Theology*, 395; a similar point is made by Sanders, *Paul and Palestinian Judaism*, 434–42.

Chapter 5: The Righteousness of God

1. The oddity and abruptness of this statement have led some to conclude that Paul was quoting a hymnic or liturgical fragment, though many others attribute it entirely to Paul. Whatever the origin of the statement, its meaning is obscure. For a survey of opinions see John Reumann, *"Righteousness" in the New Testament* (Philadelphia: Fortress, 1982), 33–35.

2. The Greek word *dikaiosynē*, translated "righteousness," "justification," or "justice," appears 58 times in the Pauline and deutero-Pauline letters. It occurs 34 times in Romans alone, but at least once in eight other letters. It is absent from Colossians, 1 and 2 Thessalonians, and Philemon.

3. Lloyd Gaston urges openness to the possibility that at least some of the references to righteousness that are not specifically identified as *God's* righteousness do in fact refer to it ("For *All* the Believers: The Inclusion of Gentiles as the Ultimate Goal of Torah in Romans," in *Paul and the Torah* [Vancouver: University of British Colombia Press, 1987], 116–34, esp. 117). This presents an interesting exegetical challenge, but it is beyond the scope of this essay to attempt it.

4. There is widespread agreement on this. See, e.g., Ernst Käsemann, "'The Righteousness of God' in Paul," in *New Testament Questions of Today* (Philadelphia: Fortress, 1969), 168–82, esp. 168; Sam K. Williams, "The 'Righteousness of God' in Romans," *JBL* 99.2 (1980): 241–90, esp. 241; A. Katherine Grieb, *The Story of Romans: A Narrative Defense of God's Righteousness* (Louisville: Westminster John Knox, 2002), passim.

5. This translation strains the category of the "objective genitive," which more appropriately designates the direct object of the action of the primary noun, and some drop this option altogether (see Marion L. Soards, "The Righteousness of God in the Writings of the Apostle Paul," *BTB* 15.3 [1985]: 104–9, esp. 104).

6. See n. 2 above. The translation "righteousness" emphasizes the quality or status of being righteous or upright. When used of humans in Paul's letters, it designates a status of conformity to the norm of God's will and thus of acceptability to God. The translation "justification" refers to God's action of declaring a person to be in the right, that is, in right relationship with God. "Justice" emphasizes legal rectitude. Leander E. Keck prefers the terms "rectification" (instead of "justification"), "rectitude" (instead of "righteousness" or "justice"), and "rectify" (for the verb) to underscore more clearly the semantic connection among these words (*Paul and His Letters* [2nd ed.; Proclamation Commentaries; Philadelphia: Fortress, 1988], 110–16).

7. Rudolf Bultmann, *Theology of the New Testament* (2 vols.; New York: Scribner's, 1951–55), 1:285.

8. Käsemann, "Righteousness of God," 169.

9. I am using the categories outlined above; Käsemann used a different classification scheme.

10. Käsemann's essay first appeared in 1961 ("Gottesgerechtigkeit bei Paulus," *ZTK* 58.3 [1961]: 367–78). The debate continued with Bultmann's response ("ΔΙΚΑΙΟΣΥΝΗ ΘΕΟΥ," *JBL* 83.1 [1964]: 12–17) and Käsemann's rebuttal, presented in the footnotes of the English translation of his essay "Righteousness of God."

11. See the summary ("Perspectives on 'God's Righteousness' in Recent German Discussion") by Manfred T. Brauch, in E. P. Sanders, *Paul and Palestinian Judaism* (Philadelphia: Fortress, 1977), 523–42.

12. See the excellent survey by John J. Scullion, "Righteousness (OT)," *ABD* 5:724–36.

13. The words *ʾĕmûnâ* and especially *ʾĕmet* also carry the meaning of "truth" and are so trans-

lated in the REB. See James Barr, *The Semantics of Biblical Language* (Oxford: Oxford University Press, 1961), 187–200.

14. Scullion, "Righteousness (OT)," 733.

15. The same words are translated "justice" by the NAB; the NJB has "justice" in v. 5 and "saving justice" in vv. 6 and 8; the REB translates "victory" in v. 5 and "saving power" in vv. 6 and 8.

16. Williams, "Righteousness of God," 261; emphasis in the original. Williams was referring to the Psalms, but his comments seem equally relevant to Deutero-Isaiah.

17. Scullion, "Righteousness (OT)," 734.

18. See Barr, *Semantics*, 263–87.

19. See Nils A. Dahl, "The Doctrine of Justification: Its Social Function and Implications," in *Studies in Paul* (Minneapolis: Augsburg, 1977), 95–120.

20. The translations are those of Geza Vermes, *The Dead Sea Scrolls in English* (4th ed.; Sheffield: Sheffield Academic Press, 1995), 86–88.

21. So Williams, "Righteousness of God," 260; James D. G. Dunn, *The Theology of Paul the Apostle* (Grand Rapids: Eerdmans, 1998), 343.

22. It should go without saying, but it is worth saying anyway, that "righteousness" is an inherently *relational* term in all these writings. It implies, e.g., human actions that are properly related to a norm, or God's actions appropriate to a covenant relationship.

23. The phrase contains a preposition (Greek *ek*) that specifies, in a way that the genitive construction does not, that the righteousness in view is "from" God. Bultmann assumed that the two phrases are interchangeable.

24. See the discussion above on Isa 51. To be fair, Käsemann uses various formulations to define the relationship between God's righteousness and power, but he does explicitly claim that "δικαιοσύνη θεοῦ appears in Rom. 1.17; 10.3ff. in personified form as Power" ("Righteousness of God," 169).

25. Käsemann concludes his essay with these words: "His doctrine of the δικαιοσύνη θεοῦ demonstrates this: God's power reaches out for the world, and the world's salvation lies in its being recaptured for the sovereignty of God. For this very reason it is the gift of God and also the salvation of the individual human being when we become obedient to the divine righteousness" ("Righteousness of God," 181–82). That is a lot of meaning for a single phrase to bear (see Barr, *Semantics*, 206–87).

26. See excursus, 66–69, below, for a discussion of justification.

27. These categories overlap, for the conduct acceptable to God flows from the gift.

28. Williams, "Righteousness of God," 263; Keck defines it similarly: "the constancy, consistency, dependability, trustworthiness, faithfulness of God," which is all summed up as "the moral integrity of God" (*Paul*, 111).

29. This is the basic understanding that Williams ascribes to the Psalms ("Righteousness of God," 262–63).

30. The NRSV reads "*through* faith for faith" and "The one who is righteous will live *by* faith." The words "through" and "by" translate the same Greek preposition *ek*, which normally means "out of" or "from" (so, e.g., NAB; James D. G. Dunn, *Romans 1–8* [WBC 38A; Dallas: Word, 1988], 37).

31. In the Psalms God's power is often evoked by descriptions of powerful deeds (e.g., Ps 33:4–6) or references to "wonders" (*niplāʾôt*) (see, e.g., 98:1–3).

32. For a good discussion of the arguments (and scholars) in favor of this interpretation, see Dunn, *Romans 1–8*, 43–44; see also Richard B. Hays, "ΠΙΣΤΙΣ and Pauline Christology:

What Is at Stake?" in *Pauline Theology*, vol. 4, *Looking Back, Pressing On* (ed. E. E. Johnson and D. M. Hay; SBLSymS 4; Atlanta: Scholars Press, 1997), 35–60, esp. 41–42; Gaston, *Paul*, 118.

33. Gaston suggests (and defends) this provocative translation (*Paul*, 118).

34. Ibid., 119.

35. The exact correspondence between error and punishment that is suggested by the Greek text is obscured in most English translations. A more literal translation of v. 28 reads: "Since they did not see *fit* to acknowledge God, God handed them over to an *unfit* mind." See Jouette M. Bassler, *Divine Impartiality: Paul and a Theological Axiom* (SBLDS 59; Chico, CA: Scholars Press, 1982), 128–29.

36. There is general, but not universal, agreement with this analysis; see Dunn, *Romans 1–8*, 51. For a different view see Stanley K. Stowers, *A Rereading of Romans: Justice, Jews, and Gentiles* (New Haven: Yale University Press, 1994), 83–125.

37. Thus scholars are unable to agree on how the summarizing comment in v. 9 should be translated: "What then? Are we [Jews?] any better off? No, not at all" (NRSV) or "What then? Are we [Jews?] at any disadvantage? No, not at all" (NRSV textual note). Other proposals include "What then do we [Jews] plead in our defense?" (Dunn, *Romans 1–8*, 144; Gaston, *Paul*, 121), and "Well then, are we better off? Not entirely" (NAB).

38. See Gaston, *Paul*, 121.

39. Cf. Gal 3:15, 17; 4:24.

40. Williams, "Righteousness of God," 270.

41. The importance of this section is described in various ways. C. E. B. Cranfield unambiguously declares it to be "the centre and heart of the whole of Rom 1.16b—15.13" (*Romans: A Shorter Commentary* [Grand Rapids: Eerdmans, 1985], 68); Dunn, too, speaks of the "centrality" of the passage, but in less emphatic terms (*Romans 1–8*, 163); Grieb does not ascribe to it the unique importance that Cranfield and Dunn do, but she does give it relative significance as "the first rhetorical climax" (*Story*, 35).

42. Paul uses different Greek words (*apokalyptetai* in 1:17; *pephanerōtai* in 3:21), but they are synonyms.

43. In Deuteronomy the exodus is described as God's redemption of Israel from slavery in Egypt (e.g., Deut 7:8), and Deutero-Isaiah repeatedly celebrates the redemption of the exiled Israelites from Babylon (e.g., Isa 43:1).

44. The opening words, "But now," establish the contrast with great emphasis.

45. Williams lists several of the proposals that have been made: "the righteousness of God [is mediated, is apprehended, is received, or is obtained] through faith in Christ" ("Righteousness of God," 272).

46. So, e.g., Williams, ibid.; Hays, "ΠΙΣΤΙΣ," 45.

47. The plausibility of this interpretation—even as a starting point in Paul's argument—seems largely overlooked by scholars, who push toward answers that emerge later in the passage or that are constructed out of theological components found outside the passage (see, e.g., Williams, "Righteousness of God," 276; Hays, "ΠΙΣΤΙΣ," 44–47). There are, of course, deeper layers here as well. Jesus' faithfulness stands in contrast to the faithlessness of some Jews (3:3) and the inexcusable and faithless behavior of Gentiles (1:18–31); but these contrasts have less direct connections with the disclosure of God's righteousness that is announced here.

48. I have made a number of exegetical decisions in rendering the verse in this way. None, I think, is irresponsible. See Sam K. Williams, *Jesus' Death as Saving Event: The Background and Origin of a Concept* (HDR 2; Missoula, MT: Scholars Press, 1975), 34–51.

49. The reference to "sins previously committed" may indicate that Paul has Gentiles in mind here; see ibid., 19–34. For a different view see Dunn, *Romans 1–8*, 173. There is general agreement that Paul is citing and reworking a pre-Pauline formula here, and the intermingling of traditional language and Pauline revisions contributes to the difficulties of the passage.

50. Greek *endeixis*, meaning "indication," "proof," or "demonstration." The same word is used in v. 25, where the NRSV translates it "show." Paul is still talking about the *manifestation* of God's righteousness.

51. The message would be that "God is righteous even in justifying the one who believes in Jesus" (so Cranfield, *Shorter Romans*, 72).

52. See Hays, "ΠΙΣΤΙΣ," 47.

53. Williams refers to "passing over" as God's "*inactivity*" (*Jesus' Death*, 29) or "self-restraint" (32).

54. This boasting is sometimes seen, especially in the older commentaries, as boasting in the salvation that one earns by one's own works (so Cranfield, *Shorter Romans*, 77), but the interpretation presented here has strong scholarly support (see the survey in Dunn, *Romans 1–8*, 185).

55. The Genesis texts speak of possessing the land (of Canaan), not of inheriting the world (Gen 15:7; 17:8). Paul's subsequent emphasis on life from death (Rom 4:17, 19, 24–25) seems to interpret this as inheriting the world to come.

56. So essentially Williams, "Righteousness of God," 278–80; see also James D. G. Dunn, "Did Paul Have a Covenant Theology? Reflections on Romans 9:4 and 11:27," in *Celebrating Romans: Template for Pauline Theology* (ed. S. E. McGinn; Grand Rapids: Eerdmans, 2004), 3–19.

57. Grieb (*Story*) tracks the theme throughout these chapters; Williams ("Righteousness of God") does so more selectively.

58. The NRSV reads, "being ignorant of the *righteousness that comes from God*," but the phrase in question is the genitive construction that is translated elsewhere in the letter, and even later in the same verse, as "God's righteousness." The NJB, e.g., correctly translates "God's saving justice."

59. This interpretation is encouraged by the NRSV's translation of the phrase as a genitive of origin. It is also promoted by Bultmann, *Theology*, 1:267; Cranfield, *Shorter Romans*, 252; and many others.

60. For examples of this line of interpretation, see James D. G. Dunn, *Romans 9–16* (WBC 38B; Dallas: Word, 1988), 595; and Williams, "Righteousness of God," 281–84; Gaston, *Paul*, 126–30.

61. Paul's purpose in writing this letter is not self-evident; see the essays in Karl P. Donfried, ed., *The Romans Debate* (rev. ed.; Peabody, MA: Hendrickson, 1991). Many, if not most, current discussions of his purpose include anticipation of the impending Jerusalem council and his defense there of his law-free Gentile churches. See, e.g., Leander E. Keck, "Romans: Introduction," in *The HarperColllins Study Bible* (ed. W. A. Meeks et al.; New York: HarperCollins, 1993), 2114–15.

62. Albert Schweitzer, *The Mysticism of Paul the Apostle* (New York: Henry Holt, 1931), 225. Among others, Krister Stendahl agrees (*Paul among Jews and Gentiles* [Philadelphia: Fortress, 1976], 84 n. 10), as does Sanders (*Paul and Palestinian Judaism*, 434-42).

63. Nils A. Dahl, "The Doctrine of Justification: Its Social Function and Implication," in *Studies in Paul* (Minneapolis: Augsburg, 1977), 95–120.

64. See, e.g., Seyoon Kim, *Paul and the New Perspective: Second Thoughts on the Origin of Paul's*

Gospel (Grand Rapids: Eerdmans, 2002). Kim sounds rather alarmist when he charges that "with its radical interpretation of Paul's gospel, especially his doctrine of justification, . . . the New Perspective School is in many respects overturning the Reformation interpretation of Paul's gospel. The potential significance of the school for the whole Christian faith can hardly be exaggerated" (xiv).

65. Dunn, *Theology*, 344. Victor P. Furnish seeks to bridge the gap between imputed and imparted righteousness within a juridical (i.e., forensic) framework through the analogy of an acquitted offender being placed within a rehabilitating situation. The analogy breaks down, however, when the rehabilitation (transformation) is ascribed to human institutions (*Theology and Ethics in Paul* [Nashville: Abingdon, 1968], 152).

66. Here "grace" does not describe the *graciousness* (freedom) of God's act of justifying but the *favor* in God's sight in which the justified person stands.

67. This characteristic and morally significant tension in Paul's letters between what is "already" the status of believers and what is "not yet" theirs is referred to as "eschatological tension" or the "eschatological reservation" (see Dunn, *Theology*, 461–98).

68. Stendahl, *Paul*, 83–84; see also Dahl, "Doctrine of Justification," 105–13; Dunn, *Theology*, 501.

Chapter 6: The Future of "Israel"

1. James D. G. Dunn, *The Theology of Paul the Apostle* (Grand Rapids: Eerdmans, 1998), 506.
2. See Peter Richardson, "The Sects of Judaism and 'True Israel,'" in *Israel in the Apostolic Church* (SNTSMS 10; Cambridge: Cambridge University Press, 1969), 217–28 (appendix C).
3. The italicized words (Greek *eis telos*) can also be translated "finally," "in the end," "until the end," "forever," or "fully." The severity of the condemnation seems different with the different translations (see, e.g., REB, NAB).
4. Nils A. Dahl, "The Future of Israel," in *Studies in Paul* (Minneapolis: Augsburg, 1977), 137–58, esp. 137; Richard H. Bell, *The Irrevocable Call of God* (WUNT 184; Tübingen: Mohr Siebeck, 2005), 71.
5. See Earl J. Richard, *First and Second Thessalonians* (SP 11; Collegeville, MN: Liturgical Press, 1995), 123–27; also Birger A. Pearson, "1 Thessalonians 2:13–16: A Deutero-Pauline Interpolation," *HTR* 64.1 (1971): 79–94; Lloyd Gaston, "Israel's Misstep in the Eyes of Paul," in *Paul and the Torah* (Vancouver: University of British Columbia Press, 1987), 135–50, esp. 137.
6. So, e.g., Bell, *Irrevocable Call*, 61.
7. So dubbed by F. D. Gilliard, "The Problem of the Antisemitic Comma Between 1 Thessalonians 2.14 and 15," *NTS* 35.4 (1989): 481–502.
8. This is not as arbitrary as it seems. The original Greek text has very little punctuation throughout and no comma here. The placement of the comma is thus a later addition, and perhaps a mistake. Without it, the condemnation falls only on those Jews who actually killed and persecuted. See Abraham J. Malherbe, *The Letters to the Thessalonians* (AB 32B; New York: Doubleday, 2000), 169; also Richardson, *Israel*, 106.
9. It is unwise to assume that 3:18–19 sheds further light on their identity, for Paul makes no effort to identify the "enemies of the cross" with the "dogs" and seems to have a different group in mind (so Gordon D. Fee, *Paul's Letter to the Philippians* [NICNT; Grand Rapids: Eerdmans, 1995], 366–75).
10. So, e.g., Richardson, *Israel*, 113.

11. See Gaston, *Paul*, 137.
12. So, e.g., Bell, *Irrevocable Call*, 181.
13. Richardson mentions, but does not embrace, this possibility (*Israel*, 113).
14. This is Richardson's conclusion (ibid., 117).
15. Gordon Fee asserts in his commentary on this passage that "God's new people are the true Israel of God," though the evidence he provides for this comes from other texts (Gordon D. Fee, *The First Epistle to the Corinthians* [NICNT; Grand Rapids: Eerdmans, 1987], 444; see also Hans Conzelmann, *1 Corinthians* [Hermeneia; Philadelphia: Fortress, 1975], 165). Quite different is Richard A. Horsley's interpretation (*1 Corinthians* [ANTC; Nashville: Abingdon, 1998], 137–39).
16. The "new covenant" language in the institution of the Lord's Supper, which Paul is quoting here, alludes to the tradition of a *renewed* covenant between Israel and Israel's God. See N. T. Wright, *The New Testament and the People of God* (Christian Origins and the Question of God 1; Minneapolis: Fortress, 1992), 301; Joel B. Green, *The Gospel of Luke* (NICNT; Grand Rapids: Eerdmans, 1997), 763.
17. So too Bell, *Irrevocable Call*, 189–90; more cautiously, Richardson, *Israel*, 122.
18. Canonical 2 Corinthians probably comprises several letters, which were combined into one sometime after Paul's death. The composite nature of the document does not affect the interpretation of 2 Cor 3.
19. See Lloyd Gaston, "Paul and the Torah in 2 Corinthians 3," in *Paul*, 151–68, esp. 152.
20. Gaston's exegesis of this passage, which removes all traces of supersession, is based on a "hermeneutic of experimentation" as he attempts to reconstruct the opponents' words. He seems to recognize that not everyone will be persuaded by his argument, but he hopes at least to make them "uneasy" about traditional readings that result in supersessionist claims (ibid., 167).
21. So, e.g., Ralph P. Martin, *2 Corinthians* (WBC 40; Waco: Word, 1986), 73; Victor P. Furnish, *II Corinthians* (AB 32A; Garden City, NY: Doubleday, 1984), 229; Richardson, *Israel*, 119. Oddly, Bell denies it (*Irrevocable Call*, 180).
22. Verse 14 is ambiguous; it could be the veil that is set aside. But for good reasons Furnish concludes that Paul is referring here to the annulment of the old covenant (*II Corinthians*, 210).
23. The Greek text reads "whenever he [or "she," there is no gender-specifying pronoun] turns to the Lord" (see REB). Dahl takes that as a reference to Moses ("Future," 137–38), but most agree that Paul had a representative Israelite in mind and the passage thus refers to the conversion of "all Israel" (so Karl Kertelge, "Letter and Spirit in 2 Corinthians 3," in *Paul and the Mosaic Law* [ed. J. D. G. Dunn; Grand Rapids: Eerdmans, 1996], 117–30, esp. 127; see also Bell, *Irrevocable Call*, 243). Whether "the Lord" is Christ (as in v. 14) or God (as in Exod 34:34, quoted here) is debated. Furnish claims that it makes little difference, since turning to God means, to Paul, accepting the gospel of Christ (*II Corinthians*, 234–35).
24. See J. Louis Martyn, *Galatians* (AB 33A; New York: Doubleday, 1997), 447–49 (Comment #45).
25. Bell, *Irrevocable Call*, 176–77; his footnotes list supporters of this view.
26. Martyn, *Galatians*, 457–66 (Comment #46).
27. Ibid., 451–57; also Sam K. Williams, *Galatians* (ANTC; Nashville: Abingdon, 1997), 130.
28. Martyn, *Galatians*, 18, 126, 459–66.

29. Ibid., 466; so also Gaston, "Israel's Enemies in Pauline Theology," in *Paul*, 80–99, esp. 90; John G. Gager, *Reinventing Paul* (Oxford: Oxford University Press, 2000), 96; Franz Mussner, *Der Galaterbrief* (HTKNT 9; Freiburg: Herder, 1981), 332.
30. The ambiguity lies in the Greek word *kai*, which can link two items (X *and* Y) or explain one item in terms of another (X, *that is*, Y).
31. Bell, *Irrevocable Call*, 180.
32. Martyn, *Galatians*, 576.
33. So Richardson, *Israel*, 82.
34. If this is the case, it amounts to solving one puzzle with another puzzle (see below on Rom 9–11).
35. Williams, *Galatians*, 167.
36. The name "Israel" appears eleven times in Rom 9–11, and "Israelite" appears twice; neither appears anywhere else in the letter. "Israel" appears only five times in all the other Pauline letters.
37. Attempts have been made to identify the "elect" as Gentiles (drawing on the argument of 9:30–31) or as faithful Jews and Gentiles (drawing on 9:30 and 11:5); but v. 7 is obviously summarizing the argument of 11:1–6, which requires the identification of the "elect" as faithful Jews.
38. For a discussion of these options see John G. Lodge, *Romans 9–11: A Reader-Response Analysis* (ISFCJ 6; Atlanta: Scholars Press, 1996), 147.
39. The alternative translation in the NRSV textual note is more severely worded: "neither will he spare you"; see also REB.
40. Some translate the text differently: "a partial hardening has come upon Israel" (so Gaston, *Paul*, 143; see also Bell, *Irrevocable Call*, 257). The context, however, strongly supports the traditional reading.
41. But see Leander E. Keck, *Romans* (ANTC; Nashville: Abingdon, 2005), 279.
42. This interpretation is strongly argued by François Refoulé, «. . . *et ainsi tout Israël sera sauvé»: Romains 11,25–32* (LD 117; Paris: Cerf, 1984).
43. This interpretation has been strongly supported in the past, but it has few adherents now; see James D. G. Dunn, *Romans 9–16* (WBC 38B; Dallas: Word, 1988), 681; Bell, *Irrevocable Call*, 260. Neither Dunn nor Bell supports this view, but they both discuss it.
44. Some take this to mean every individual Israelite (so Bell, *Irrevocable Call*, 262), but the direction of Paul's argument places the emphasis on the reunification of the two *groups* (so, e.g., Dahl, "Future," 153; Dunn, *Theology*, 527).
45. An important variant of this interpretation is given by Mary Ann Getty ("Paul and the Salvation of Israel: A Perspective on Romans 9–11," *CBQ* 50.4 [1988]: 459). Her interpretation includes the insights of (3) but, like (2), includes Gentiles in "Israel." However, she claims that Paul applies the name "Israel" to an entity *expanded* by the inclusion of Gentiles, not (as in [2]) to one diminished by the *exclusion* of most Jews.
46. Most English translations obscure this by translating the words differently in the two places, but see REB.
47. Within Rom 9–11, the last reference to Christ is in 10:17.
48. "Israel must come to faith in Christ in order to be saved" (Bell, *Irrevocable Call*, 268). The same conclusion is drawn by Keck, *Romans*, 282; Bruce W. Longenecker, "Different Answers to Different Issues: Israel, the Gentiles and Salvation History in Romans 9–11," *JSNT* 36 (1989): 95–123; Dunn, *Romans 9–16*, 683; Murray Baker, "Paul and the Salva-

tion of Israel: Paul's Ministry, the Motif of Jealousy, and Israel's Yes," *CBQ* 67.3 (2005): 482; and others.

49. Verse 23 refers to Israel's *apistia*, which the NRSV translates "unbelief." The word, however, can mean "faithlessness" (i.e., to God) and does not necessarily mean disbelief *in Christ* (see chap. 3, above).

50. So Gaston, *Paul*, 148.

51. This line of interpretation requires new and creative—but not implausible—readings of passages that have for centuries been interpreted quite differently; see, e.g., Stanley K. Stowers, *A Rereading of Romans: Justice, Jews, and Gentiles* (New Haven: Yale University Press, 1994), 285–316; also Gager, *Reinventing Paul*, 102–43, esp. 128–42; Franz Mussner, *Tractate on the Jews* (Philadelphia: Fortress, 1984), 28–36; Krister Stendahl, *Paul among Jews and Gentiles* (Philadelphia: Fortress, 1976), 4 (though Stendahl modifies, or clarifies, his position somewhat in *Final Account: Paul's Letter to the Romans* [Minneapolis: Fortress, 1995], x).

52. Dunn, *Theology*, 528; similarly Getty, "Paul," 469.

53. Calvin J. Roetzel, *Paul: A Jew on the Margins* (Louisville: Westminster John Knox, 2003), 86.

54. Lodge (*Romans 9–11*) imaginatively constructs the interpretations of Rom 9–11 that readers with different presuppositions would develop.

55. Bell, *Irrevocable Call*, 415–16.

56. Ibid., 414–15.

57. Gaston, "A Retrospective Introduction," in *Paul*, 1–14, esp. 2.

58. Gaston, *Paul*, 148.

59. Stendahl, *Final Account*, 40.

60. Charles H. Cosgrove, *Elusive Israel: The Puzzle of Election in Romans* (Louisville: Westminster John Knox, 1997), 38–39, emphasis his; see also Lodge, *Romans 9–11*, 90 n. 29.

61. Lodge, *Romans 9–11*, 216.

Chapter 7: "Then Comes the End . . ."

1. See Wayne A. Meeks, "Social Functions of Apocalyptic Language in Pauline Christianity," in *Apocalypticism in the Mediterranean World and the Near East* (ed. D. Hellholm; Tübingen: Mohr [Siebeck], 1983) 687–705; John G. Gager, "Functional Diversity in Paul's Use of End-Time Language," *JBL* 89.3 (1970): 325–37.

2. See 1 Thess 4:13–5:11; 1 Cor 15:12–57; 2 Cor 5:1–10; Phil 1:21–24; 3:20–21; Rom 8:18–25. Because its authorship is uncertain, I do not include 2 Thess 1:5–2:12 in this survey.

3. According to Josephus, the Pharisees believed in life after death but the Sadducees did not (*War* 2.8.14 §§162–66; *Ant.* 18.1.3–4 §§12–17; see also Acts 23:8). The Dead Sea Scrolls reflect the views of an apocalyptic sect, usually identified as the Essenes. See Alan F. Segal, *Life after Death: A History of the Afterlife in the Religions of the West* (New York: Doubleday, 2004), ad loc.

4. See Segal, *Life after Death*, 134–45.

5. This view goes back at least to Plato, though it is not clear whether it was widespread outside philosophical circles. Abraham Malherbe thinks that it was; see *The Letters to the Thessalonians* (AB 32B; New York: Doubleday, 2000), 281–83. For a full discussion of these classical views, see Segal, *Life after Death*, 204–47.

6. In what follows I am indebted to the analyses of George W. E. Nickelsburg, *Resurrection*,

Immortality, and Eternal Life in Intertestamental Judaism (HTS 26; Cambridge: Harvard University Press, 1972).

7. The Greek tradition speaks of the "soul"; in Hellenistic Jewish writings "soul" (*psychē*) and "spirit" (*pneuma*) are sometimes used interchangeably (see Segal, *Life after Death*, esp. 142–45, 351–87).

8. Or the bodies of *some of* the dead. Daniel 12 asserts only that *some* will arise, referring apparently to those who had been unjustly slaughtered during the persecution of Antiochus IV (ca. 167 BCE) and to their hellenizing oppressors, who will be raised for their respective rewards and punishments. Similarly, the *Testament of Judah* assumes that only martyrs will experience resurrection (25:4). See Nickelsburg, *Resurrection*, 23, 35.

9. Ibid., 24; see also Segal, *Life after Death*, 285–94.

10. Nickelsburg, *Resurrection*, 180.

11. There are various ways of reconstructing the situation, but this is the most widely accepted; see Malherbe, *Thessalonians*, 283–85; Earl J. Richard, *First and Second Thessalonians* (SP 11; Collegeville, MN: Liturgical Press, 1995), 231–32.

12. There is no specific reference to a *bodily* assumption in these verses, but it is later implied (see 5:23).

13. The translation is that of *The Old Testament Pseudepigrapha*, vol. 1, *Apocalyptic Literature and Testaments* (ed. J. H. Charlesworth; New York: Doubleday, 1983), 552.

14. The issues are (1) whether this is a remembered word of the earthly Jesus or a special revelation of the risen Christ, and (2) how far the reported word extends (to v. 15 or to vv. 16–17?). See Malherbe, *Thessalonians*, 267–71.

15. See esp. Richard, *Thessalonians*, 242.

16. Malherbe (*Thessalonians*, 280–81) and Charles A. Wanamaker (*The Epistles to the Thessalonians* [NIGTC; Grand Rapids: Eerdmans, 1990], 167) insist that the language of sleep is purely metaphorical; Margaret E. Thrall presumes that Paul intends to suggest postmortem unconsciousness (*The Second Epistle to the Corinthians* [ICC; Edinburgh: T & T Clark, 1994], 1:398).

17. Most think the movement will be back to heaven, but I. Howard Marshall argues that Paul envisions the whole entourage descending to a new earth (*1 and 2 Thessalonians* [NCB; Grand Rapids: Eerdmans, 1983], 124–25).

18. Meeks, "Social Functions," 693.

19. So Richard A. Horsley, *1 Corinthians* (ANTC; Nashville: Abingdon, 1998), 200–203.

20. So Gordon D. Fee, *The First Epistle to the Corinthians* (NICNT; Grand Rapids: Eerdmans, 1987), 715; Meeks, "Social Functions," 698–700.

21. The key verse here is 5:3, which contains a significant textual variant. Some Greek manuscripts refer to being unclothed and the wish not to be found naked (the NRSV and NAB reflect this reading); others refer to being clothed and thus not naked (the REB and NJB reflect this reading). My analysis follows the NRSV.

22. So, e.g., Barnabas Lindars, "The Sound of the Trumpet: Paul and Eschatology," *BJRL* 67.2 (1984–85): 776–78; Charles K. Barrett, *The Second Epistle to the Corinthians* (HNTC; New York: Harper & Row, 1973), 153; more cautiously James D. G. Dunn, *The Theology of Paul the Apostle* (Grand Rapids: Eerdmans, 1998), 489–90.

23. So, e.g., Thrall, *Second Epistle*, 370. Alternatively, the present tense verb ("we have") could indicate certainty regarding the existence of the spiritual body without implying immediate possession of it. For a careful evaluation of all alternative hypotheses, see ibid., 357–70.

24. See ibid., 378–79.
25. So, e.g., Victor P. Furnish, *II Corinthians* (AB 32A; New York: Doubleday, 1984), 297–99.
26. Thrall, *Second Epistle*, 379 (following the reading of the REB and NJB); see also Calvin J. Roetzel, *Paul: A Jew on the Margins* (Louisville: Westminster John Knox, 2003), 40.
27. Gordon Fee recognizes most clearly the tension here (see *Paul's Letter to the Philippians* [NICNT; Grand Rapids: Eerdmans, 1995], 149 n. 48). He attributes it to the inherent tension between the spatial (heaven and earth) and temporal (this age and the age to come) categories in Paul's eschatology.
28. In 2 Cor 4:14–5:11 "we" refers primarily to Paul but clearly embraces others as well (5:5, 10); see Thrall, *Second Epistle*, 398.
29. This possibility is hinted at by Segal (*Life after Death*, 424).
30. There are intense debates over whether Paul refers only to the inanimate world when he speaks of "the whole creation" or intends to include all humanity in the phrase. Dunn thinks that Paul has nonhuman creation primarily in mind (James D. G. Dunn, *Romans 1–8* [WBC 38A; Dallas: Word, 1988], 469–70), but Keck notes that "humans are an integral part of creation." If that is the case, then "Paul implies more than he actually says" (Leander E. Keck, *Romans* [ANTC; Nashville: Abingdon, 2005], 210).

Bibliography

Achtemeier, Paul J. "Apropos the Faith of/in Christ." In *Pauline Theology*, vol. 4, *Looking Back, Pressing On*, edited by E. E. Johnson and D. M. Hay, 82–92. SBLSymS 4. Atlanta: Scholars Press, 1997.

Ashton, John. *The Religion of Paul the Apostle*. New Haven: Yale University Press, 2000.

Badenas, Robert. *Christ the End of the Law: Romans 10.4 in Pauline Perspective*. JSNTSup 10. Sheffield: JSOT Press, 1985.

Baker, Murray. "Paul and the Salvation of Israel: Paul's Ministry, the Motif of Jealousy, and Israel's Yes." *CBQ* 67.3 (2005): 469–84.

Barclay, John M. G. "'Neither Jew nor Greek': Multiculturalism and the New Perspective on Paul." In *Ethnicity and the Bible*, edited by M. G. Brett, 197–214. Biblical Interpretation Series 19. Leiden: Brill, 1996.

Barcley, William B. *"Christ in You": A Study in Paul's Theology and Ethics*. Lanham, MD: University Press of America, 1999.

Barr, James. *The Semantics of Biblical Language*. Oxford: Oxford University Press, 1961.

Barrett, Charles K. *The Second Epistle to the Corinthians*. HNTC. New York: Harper & Row, 1973.

Bassler, Jouette M. *Divine Impartiality: Paul and a Theological Axiom*. SBLDS 59. Chico, CA: Scholars Press, 1982.

———. "The Problem of Self-Definition: What 'Self' and Whose Definition?" In *Redefining First-Century Jewish and Christian Identities: Essays in Honor of Ed P. Sanders*, edited by F. E. Udoh. Notre Dame, IN: University of Notre Dame Press, forthcoming 2006.

Beasley-Murray, George R. *Baptism in the New Testament*. Grand Rapids: Eerdmans, 1962.

Becker, Jürgen. *Paul: Apostle to the Gentiles*. Louisville: Westminster John Knox, 1993.

Beker, J. Christiaan. *Paul the Apostle: The Triumph of God in Life and Thought*. Philadelphia: Fortress, 1980.

Bell, Richard H. *The Irrevocable Call of God*. WUNT 184. Tübingen: Mohr Siebeck, 2005.

Betz, Hans D. "Transferring a Ritual: Paul's Interpretation of Baptism in Romans 6." In *Paul in His Hellenistic Context*, edited by T. Engberg-Pedersen, 84–118. Edinburgh: T. & T. Clark, 1994.

Boers, Hendrikus. "Ἀγάπη and χάρις in Paul's Thought." *CBQ* 59.4 (1997): 693–713.

Borgen, Peder. *Paul Preaches Circumcision and Pleases Men and Other Essays on Christian Origins*. Trondheim: TAPIR, 1983.

———. *Philo, John, and Paul: New Perspectives on Judaism and Early Christianity*. Brown Judaic Studies 131. Atlanta: Scholars Press, 1987.

Bornkamm, Günther. *Paul*. New York: Harper & Row, 1971.

Bousset, Wilhelm. *Kyrios Christos*. Göttingen: Vandenhoeck & Ruprecht, 1913. ET, *Kyrios Christos*. Nashville: Abingdon, 1970.

Bouttier, Michel. *En Christ: Étude d'exégèse et de théologie pauliennes*. Paris: Presses Universitaires de France, 1962.

Boyarin, Daniel. *A Radical Jew: Paul and the Politics of Identity*. Berkeley: University of California Press, 1994.

Brauch, Manfred T. "Perspectives on 'God's Righteousness' in Recent German Discussion." In *Paul and Palestinian Judaism*, by E. P. Sanders, 523–42. Philadelphia: Fortress, 1977.

Bultmann, Rudolf. "ΔΙΚΑΙΟΣΎΝΗ ΘΕΟΎ." *JBL* 83.1 (1964): 12–16.

———. *Theology of the New Testament*. 2 vols. New York: Scribner's, 1951–1955.

Campbell, Alastair. "Dying with Christ: The Origin of a Metaphor?" In *Baptism, the New Testament, and the Church: Historical and Contemporary Studies in Honour of R. E. O. White*, edited by S. E. Porter and A. R. Cross, 273–93. JSNTSup 171. Sheffield: Sheffield Academic Press, 1999.

Campbell, William S. *Paul's Gospel in an Intercultural Context: Jew and Gentile in the Letter to the Romans*. Studies in the Intercultural History of Christianity 69. Frankfort am Main: Lang, 1991.

Carson, Donald A., Peter T. O'Brien, and Mark A. Seifrid, eds. *Justification and Variegated Nomism*. 2 vols. Grand Rapids: Baker, 2001–2004.

Cohen, Shaye J. D. "Crossing the Boundary and Becoming a Jew." *HTR* 82.1 (1989): 13–33.

Collins, John J. "A Symbol of Otherness: Circumcision and Salvation in the First Century." In *"To See Ourselves as Others See Us": Christians, Jews, "Others" in Late Antiquity*, edited by J. Neusner and E. S. Frerichs, 163–86. Chico, CA: Scholars Press, 1985.

Conzelmann, Hans. *1 Corinthians*. Hermeneia. Philadelphia: Fortress, 1975.

———. *An Outline of the Theology of the New Testament*. New Testament Library. London: SCM, 1969.

———, and Walther Zimmerli. "Χάρις, κτλ." *TDNT* 9:359–415.

Cosgrove, Charles H. *Elusive Israel: The Puzzle of Election in Romans*. Louisville: Westminster John Knox, 1997.

Cousar, Charles B. *A Theology of the Cross: The Death of Jesus in the Pauline Letters*. OBT. Minneapolis: Fortress, 1990.

Cranfield, Charles E. B. *Romans*. 2 vols. ICC. Edinburgh: T. & T. Clark, 1975–79.

———. *Romans: A Shorter Commentary*. Grand Rapids: Eerdmans, 1985.

Crossan, John Dominic, and Jonathan L. Reed. *In Search of Paul*. San Francisco: HarperCollins, 2004.

Dahl, Nils A. "The Doctrine of Justification: Its Social Function and Implications." In *Studies in Paul*, by Nils A. Dahl, 95–120. Minneapolis: Augsburg, 1977.

———. "The Future of Israel." In *Studies in Paul*, by Nils A. Dahl, 137–58. Minneapolis: Augsburg, 1977.

Deissmann, Adolf. *Paul: A Study in Social and Religious History*. 2nd ed. New York: Doran, 1926.

Donfried, Karl P. "Justification and Last Judgment in Paul." *Int* 30.2 (1976): 140–52.

————, ed. *The Romans Debate*. Rev. ed. Peabody, MA: Hendrickson, 1991.

Drane, John W. *Paul: Libertine or Legalist?* London: SPCK, 1975.

Dunn, James D. G. "'Baptized' as Metaphor." In *Baptism, the New Testament and the Church: Historical and Contemporary Studies in Honour of R. E. O. White*, edited by S. E. Porter and A. R. Cross, 294–310. JSNTSup 171. Sheffield: Sheffield Academic Press, 1999.

————. "Did Paul Have a Covenant Theology? Reflections on Romans 9:4 and 11:27." In *Celebrating Romans: Template for Pauline Theology*, edited by S. E. McGinn, 3–19. Grand Rapids: Eerdmans, 2004.

————. "The Incident at Antioch (Gal. 2:11–18)." In *Jesus, Paul, and the Law: Studies in Mark and Galatians*, by James D. G. Dunn, 129–74. Louisville: Westminster/John Knox, 1990.

————. "The New Perspective on Paul: Paul and the Law." In *Romans 1–8*, by James D. G. Dunn, lxiii–lxxii. WBC 38A. Dallas: Word, 1988.

————. "Once More, ΠΙΣΤΙΣ ΧΡΙΣΤΟΥ." In *Pauline Theology*, vol. 4, *Looking Back, Pressing On*, edited by E. E. Johnson and D. M. Hay, 61–81. SBLSymS 4. Atlanta: Scholars Press, 1997.

————. *Romans 1–8*. WBC 38A. Dallas: Word, 1988.

————. *Romans 9–16*. WBC 38B. Dallas: Word, 1988.

————. *The Theology of Paul the Apostle*. Grand Rapids: Eerdmans, 1998.

————, ed. *Paul and the Mosaic Law*. Grand Rapids: Eerdmans, 2001.

Eastman, Brad. *The Significance of Grace in the Letters of Paul*. New York: Peter Lang, 1999.

Fatum, Lone. "Image of God and Glory of Man: Women in the Pauline Congregations." In *Image of God and Gender Models in Judaeo-Christian Tradition*, edited by K. E. Børresen, 56–137. Oslo: Solum, 1991.

Fee, Gordon D. *The First Epistle to the Corinthians*. NICNT. Grand Rapids: Eerdmans, 1987.

————. *Paul's Letter to the Philippians*. NICNT. Grand Rapids: Eerdmans, 1995.

Feske, Millicent C. "Christ and Suffering in Moltmann's Thought." *Asbury Theological Journal* 55 (2000): 85–104.

Fredriksen, Paula. "Judaism, the Circumcision of Gentiles, and Apocalyptic Hope: Another Look at Galatians 1 and 2." *JTS* 42.2 (1991): 532–64.

Furnish, Victor P. *II Corinthians*. AB 32A. Garden City, NY: Doubleday, 1984.

————. *Theology and Ethics in Paul*. Nashville: Abingdon, 1968.

Gager, John G. "Functional Diversity in Paul's Use of End-Time Language." *JBL* 89.3 (1970): 325–37.

————. *Reinventing Paul*. Oxford: Oxford University Press, 2000.

Gaston, Lloyd. *Paul and the Torah*. Vancouver: University of British Columbia Press, 1987.

Gathercole, Simon J. *Where Is Boasting? Early Jewish Soteriology and Paul's Response in Romans 1–5*. Grand Rapids: Eerdmans, 2002.

Getty, Mary Ann. "Paul and the Salvation of Israel: A Perspective on Romans 9–11." *CBQ* 50.3 (1988): 456–69.

Gilliard, F. D. "The Problem of the Antisemitic Comma Between 1 Thessalonians 2.14 and 15." *NTS* 35.4 (1989): 481–502.

Goodenough, Erwin R., and A. T. Kraabel. "Paul and the Hellenization of Christianity." In *Religions in Antiquity: Essays in Memory of Erwin R. Goodenough*, edited by J. Neusner, 23–68. SHR 14. Leiden: Brill, 1968.

Green, Joel B. *The Gospel of Luke*. NICNT. Grand Rapids: Eerdmans, 1997.

Grieb, A. Katherine. *The Story of Romans: A Narrative Defense of God's Righteousness.* Louisville: Westminster John Knox, 2002.

Gundry, Robert H. "Grace, Works, and Staying Saved in Paul." *Bib* 66.1 (1985): 1–38.

Hagner, Donald A. "Paul and Judaism: The Jewish Matrix of Early Christianity: Issues in the Current Debate." *BBR* 3 (1993): 111–30.

Hay, David M. "*Pistis* as 'Ground for Faith' in Hellenized Judaism and Paul." *JBL* 108.3 (1989): 461–76.

Hays, Richard B. *The Faith of Jesus Christ.* SBLDS 56. Chico, CA: Scholars Press, 1983.

———. "ΠΙΣΤΙΣ and Pauline Christology: What Is at Stake?" In *Pauline Theology*, vol. 4, *Looking Back, Pressing On*, edited by E. E. Johnson and D. M. Hay, 35–60. SBLSymS 4. Atlanta: Scholars Press, 1997.

Hooker, Morna D. *From Adam to Christ: Essays on Paul.* Cambridge: Cambridge University Press, 1990.

———. "Paul and 'Covenantal Nomism.'" In *Paul and Paulinism: Essays in Honour of C. K. Barrett*, edited by M. D. Hooker and S. G. Wilson, 47–56. London: SPCK, 1982.

———. "Πίστις Χριστοῦ." In *From Adam to Christ: Essays on Paul*, by Morna D. Hooker, 165–86. Cambridge: Cambridge University Press, 1990.

Horsley, Richard A. *1 Corinthians.* ANTC. Nashville: Abingdon, 1998.

Howard, George. "Faith of Christ." *ABD* 2:758–60.

———. "On the 'Faith of Christ.'" *HTR* 60.4 (1967): 459–84.

Hübner, Hans. *Law in Paul's Thought.* Edinburgh: T. & T. Clark, 1984.

Johnson, Luke T. "Rom. 3.21–26 and the Faith of Jesus." *CBQ* 44.1 (1982): 77–90.

Käsemann, Ernst. "Gottesgerechtigkeit bei Paulus." *ZTK* 58.3 (1961): 367–78. ET, "'The Righteousness of God' in Paul." In *New Testament Questions of Today*, by Ernst Käsemann, 168–82. Philadelphia: Fortress, 1969.

———. *Romans.* Grand Rapids: Eerdmans, 1980.

———. "The Theological Problem Presented by the Motif of the Body of Christ." In *Perspectives on Paul*, by Ernst Käsemann, 102–21. Philadelphia: Fortress, 1969.

Keck, Leander E. "'Jesus' in Romans." *JBL* 108.3 (1989): 443–60.

———. *Paul and His Letters.* 2nd ed. Proclamation Commentaries. Philadelphia: Fortress, 1988.

———. *Romans.* ANTC. Nashville: Abingdon, 2005.

———. "Romans: Introduction." In *The HarperCollins Study Bible*, edited by W. A. Meeks et al., 2114–15. New York: HarperCollins, 1993.

Kertelge, Karl. "Letter and Spirit in 2 Corinthians 3." In *Paul and the Mosaic Law*, edited by J. D. G. Dunn, 117–30. Grand Rapids: Eerdmans, 1996.

Kim, Seyoon. *Paul and the New Perspective: Second Thoughts on the Origin of Paul's Gospel.* Grand Rapids: Eerdmans, 2002.

Kloppenborg, John S. "Egalitarianism in the Myth and Rhetoric of Pauline Churches." In *Reimagining Christian Origins: A Colloquium Honoring Burton L. Mack*, edited by E. A. Castelli and H. Taussig, 247–63. Valley Forge, PA: Trinity Press International, 1996.

Laato, Timo. *Paul and Judaism: An Anthropological Approach.* SFSHJ 115. Atlanta: Scholars Press, 1995.

Lieu, Judith. "'Impregnable Ramparts and Walls of Iron': Boundary and Identity in Early 'Judaism' and 'Christianity.'" *NTS* 48.3 (2002): 297–313.

Lindars, Barnabas. "The Sound of the Trumpet: Paul and Eschatology." *BJRL* 67.2 (1984–85): 766–82.

Lodge, John G. *Romans 9–11: A Reader-Response Analysis*. ISFCJ 6. Atlanta: Scholars Press, 1996.

Longenecker, Bruce W. "Different Answers to Different Issues: Israel, the Gentiles and Salvation History in Romans 9–11." *JSNT* 36 (1989): 95–123.

Longenecker, Richard N. *Galatians*. WBC 41. Dallas: Word, 1990.

Lührmann, Dieter. "Faith: New Testament." *ABD* 2:749–58.

McEleney, Neil J. "Conversion, Circumcision and the Law." *NTS* 20.3 (1974): 319–41.

McGinn, Bernard. *The Foundations of Mysticism*. New York: Crossroad, 1991.

Malherbe, Abraham J. *The Letters to the Thessalonians*. AB 32B. New York: Doubleday, 2000.

Marshall, I. Howard. *1 and 2 Thessalonians*. NCB. Grand Rapids: Eerdmans, 1983.

———. "Salvation, Grace, and Works in the Later Writings in the Pauline Corpus." *NTS* 42.3 (1996): 339–58.

Martin, Dale B. *The Corinthian Body*. New Haven: Yale University Press, 1995.

Martin, Ralph P. *2 Corinthians*. WBC 40. Waco: Word, 1986.

Martyn, J. Louis. "Apocalyptic Antinomies in Paul's Letter to the Galatians." *NTS* 31.3 (1985): 410–24.

———. *Galatians*. AB 33A. New York: Doubleday, 1997.

Meeks, Wayne A. "The Social Context of Pauline Theology." *Int* 36.3 (1982): 266–77.

———. "Social Functions of Apocalyptic Language in Pauline Christianity." In *Apocalypticism in the Mediterranean World and the Near East*, edited by D. Hellholm, 687–705. Tübingen: Mohr (Siebeck), 1983.

Moffatt, James. *Grace in the New Testament*. New York: Long & Smith, 1932.

Montefiore, Claude G. *Judaism and St. Paul: Two Essays*. London: Goschen, 1914.

Moo, Douglas J. "'Law,' 'Works of the Law,' and Legalism in Paul." *WTJ* 45.1 (1983): 73–100.

Moore, George F. *Judaism in the First Centuries of the Christian Era*. 3 vols. Cambridge: Harvard University Press, 1927–30.

Moxnes, Halvor. "Social Integration and the Problem of Gender in St. Paul's Letters." *Studia theologica* 43.1 (1989): 99–113.

Mussner, Franz. *Der Galaterbrief*. HTKNT 9. Freiburg: Herder, 1981.

———. *Tractate on the Jews*. Philadelphia: Fortress, 1984.

Neyrey, Jerome H. "Bewitched in Galatia." *CBQ* 50.1 (1988): 72–100.

Nickelsburg, George W. E. *Resurrection, Immortality, and Eternal Life in Intertestamental Judaism*. HTS 26. Cambridge: Harvard University Press, 1972.

Nolland, John. "Uncircumcised Proselytes?" *JSJ* 12.2 (1981): 173–94.

O'Brien, Peter T. "Justification in Paul and Some Crucial Issues of the Last Two Decades." In *Right with God: Justification in the Bible and the World*, edited by D. A. Carson, 68–95. Grand Rapids: Baker, 1992.

Pearson, Birger A. "1 Thessalonians 2:13–16: A Deutero-Pauline Interpolation." *HTR* 64.1 (1971): 79–94.

Pearson, Brook W. R. "Baptism and Initiation in the Cult of Isis and Sarapis." In *Baptism, the New Testament and the Church: Historical and Contemporary Studies in Honour of R. E. O. White*, edited by S. E. Porter and A. O. Cross, 42–62. JSNTSup 171. Sheffield: Sheffield Academic Press, 1999.

Pelser, Gert M. M. "Could the 'Formulas' *Dying* and *Rising with Christ* Be Expressions of Pauline Mysticism?" *Neot* 32.1 (1998): 115–34.

———. "Once More the Body of Christ in Paul." *Neot* 32.2 (1998): 525–45.

Räisänen, Heikki. "Legalism and Salvation by the Law." In *The Torah and Christ*, by Heikki Räisänen, 25–54. Helsinki: Finnish Exegetical Society, 1986.

———. *Paul and the Law*. WUNT 29. Philadelphia: Fortress, 1986.

Reasoner, Mark. *Romans in Full Circle: A History of Interpretation*. Louisville: Westminster John Knox, 2005.

Refoulé, François. «. . . *et ainsi tout Israël sera sauvé»: Romains 11,25–32*. LD 117. Paris: Cerf, 1984.

Reitzenstein, Richard. *Die hellenistischen Mysterienreligionen*. Leipzig: Teubner, 1910. ET, *Hellenistic Mystery-Religions*. Pittsburgh: Pickwick, 1978.

Reumann, John. *"Righteousness" in the New Testament*. Philadelphia: Fortress, 1982.

Richard, Earl J. *First and Second Thessalonians*. SP 11. Collegeville, MN: Liturgical Press, 1995.

Richardson, Peter. *Israel in the Apostolic Church*. SNTSMS 10. Cambridge: Cambridge University Press, 1969.

Robinson, John A. T. *The Body: A Study in Pauline Theology*. SBT 1.5. London: SCM, 1952.

Roetzel, Calvin J. "'As Dying and Behold We Live': Death and Resurrection in Paul's Theology." *Int* 46.1 (1992): 5–18.

———. *Paul: A Jew on the Margins*. Louisville: Westminster John Knox, 2003.

———. *Paul: The Man and the Myth*. Columbia, SC: University of South Carolina Press, 1998.

Sanders, E. P. "Judaism and the Grand 'Christian' Abstractions: Love, Mercy, and Grace." *Int* 39.4 (1985): 357–72.

———. *Paul and Palestinian Judaism*. Philadelphia: Fortress, 1977.

———. *Paul, the Law, and the Jewish People*. Philadelphia: Fortress, 1983.

Schechter, Solomon. *Aspects of Rabbinic Theology*. 1909. Repr., New York: Schocken, 1961.

Schiffman, Lawrence H. *Who Was a Jew? Rabbinic and Halakhic Perspectives on the Jewish Christian Schism*. Hoboken, NJ: Ktav, 1985.

Schweitzer, Albert. *The Mysticism of Paul the Apostle*. New York: Henry Holt, 1931.

Scullion, J. J. "Righteousness (OT)." *ABD* 5:724–36.

Segal, Alan F. *Life after Death: A History of the Afterlife in the Religions of the West*. New York: Doubleday, 2004.

Smith, Jonathan Z. "Fences and Neighbors: Some Contours of Early Judaism." In *Imagining Religion: From Babylon to Jonestown*, by Jonathan Z. Smith, 1–18. Chicago Studies in the History of Judaism. Chicago: University of Chicago Press, 1982.

Soards, Marion L. "The Righteousness of God in the Writings of the Apostle Paul." *BTB* 15.3 (1985): 104–9.

Stendahl, Krister. "The Apostle Paul and the Introspective Conscience of the West." *HTR* 56.3 (1963): 199–215.

———. *Final Account: Paul's Letter to the Romans*. Minneapolis: Fortress, 1995.

———. *Paul among Jews and Gentiles*. Philadelphia: Fortress, 1976.

Stowers, Stanley K. *A Rereading of Romans: Justice, Jews, and Gentiles*. New Haven: Yale University Press, 1994.

Talbert, Charles H. "Paul, Judaism, and the Revisionists." *CBQ* 63.1 (2001): 1–22.

Tannehill, Robert. *Dying and Rising with Christ: A Study in Pauline Theology*. BZNW 32. Berlin: Töpelmann, 1966.

Thielman, Frank. *From Plight to Solution: A Jewish Framework for Understanding Paul's View of the Law in Galatians and Romans*. NovTSup 61. Leiden: Brill, 1989.

———. *Paul and the Law: A Contextual Approach.* Downers Grove, IL: InterVarsity, 1994.

Thrall, Margaret E. *The Second Epistle to the Corinthians.* ICC. Edinburgh: T. & T. Clark, 1994.

Vermes, Geza. *The Dead Sea Scrolls in English.* 4th ed. Sheffield: Sheffield Academic Press, 1995.

Wanamaker, Charles A. *The Epistles to the Thessalonians.* NIGTC. Grand Rapids: Eerdmans, 1990.

Watson, Francis. *Paul, Judaism, and the Gentiles.* SNTSMS 56. Cambridge: Cambridge University Press, 1986.

Westerholm, Stephen. *Israel's Law and the Church's Faith: Paul and His Recent Interpreters.* Grand Rapids: Eerdmans, 1988.

———. *Perspectives Old and New on Paul: The "Lutheran" Paul and His Critics.* Grand Rapids: Eerdmans, 2004.

Whiteley, Denys E. H. *The Theology of St. Paul.* Oxford: Blackwell, 1964.

Wiley, Tatha. *Paul and the Gentile Women: Reframing Galatians.* New York: Continuum, 2005.

Williams, Sam K. "Again *Pistis Christou.*" *CBQ* 49.3 (1987): 431–37.

———. *Galatians.* ANTC. Nashville: Abingdon, 1997.

———. *Jesus' Death as Saving Event: The Background and Origin of a Concept.* HDR 2. Missoula, MT: Scholars Press, 1975.

———. "The 'Righteousness of God' in Romans." *JBL* 99.2 (1980): 241–90.

Wilson, Stephen G. "Paul and Religion." In *Paul and Paulinism: Essays in Honour of C. K. Barrett,* edited by M. D. Hooker and S. G. Wilson, 339–54. London: SPCK, 1982.

Winger, Michael. "Act One: Paul Arrives in Galatia." *NTS* 48.4 (2002): 548–67.

———. *By What Law? The Meaning of* Νόμος *in the Letters of Paul.* SBLDS 128. Atlanta: Scholars Press, 1992.

Witt, Reginald E. *Isis in the Ancient World.* Baltimore: Johns Hopkins University Press, 1971.

Wrede, William. *Paul.* London: Phillip Green, 1907.

Wright, N. T. *The Climax of the Covenant: Christ and the Law in Pauline Theology.* Minneapolis: Fortress, 1992.

———. *The New Testament and the People of God.* Christian Origins and the Question of God 1. Minneapolis: Fortress, 1992.

Yinger, Kent L. *Paul, Judaism, and Judgment according to Deeds.* SNTSMS 105. Cambridge: Cambridge University Press, 1999.

Index of Ancient Sources

Index of Modern Authors

Index of Subjects